more
curious
questions

By the same author
Curious Questions
Curious Kiwi Words
Curious Thoughts

more curious questions

As heard
on National
Radio

Max Cryer

HarperCollins*Publishers*

National Library of New Zealand Cataloguing-in-Publication Data

Cryer, Max.
More curious questions / Max Cryer.
Includes bibliographical references.
ISBN 1-86950-475-5
1. English language—Idioms.
2. English language—Terms and phrases.
3. Questions and answers.
I. National Radio (N.Z.)
II. Title.
428.1—dc 21

First published 2003

HarperCollins*Publishers (New Zealand) Limited*
P.O. Box 1, Auckland

Copyright © Max Cryer 2003

Max Cryer asserts the moral right to be identified
as the author of this work.

ISBN 1 86950 475 5

Set in Janson Text
Designed and typeset by Janine Brougham
Printed by Griffin Press, Australia on 79 gsm Bulky Paperback

Introduction

I have been answering radio listeners' language questions for six years, and the first *Curious Questions* book received a very encouraging response. These factors have reassured me that there are many people out there who are interested in the language and who do care about it.

Research work isn't easy, but it brings satisfaction, as does the support and interest from listeners and readers. One kind person provided me with a very gratifying assessment:

'You provide enlightenment without pomposity.'

I only hope I can maintain that combination in the future, and in this book.

Max Cryer
October 2003

Computer language has made @ a common symbol — does it have a name?

Many people can recognise and name a question mark, an ampersand, a hash sign, an asterisk, a colon, a chevron and a slash. But the @ or 'squiggly at' is not so easy to pin down.

Italian academics claim that the symbol has been around since at least the 1500s. In those days it had a strong position in commerce, because grains and liquids were transported in jars that held a strictly measured amount. The jars were called *amphoras*, so the single letter 'a' signified goods of the volume of one amphora jar, and the 'a' was written with Italian flourish.

The sign settled to mean at the price of and was used that way in Europe for centuries, e.g. 3 metres of lace @ 500 lire per metre.

The @ sign took a while to get onto typewriter keyboards, but it was there by 1880 and by the 1960s it began to be carried over to computers. In 1972 the symbol was chosen to be the separator in e-mail addresses and it has been so successful that even languages like Tamil, Japanese and Arabic have taken it aboard even though they don't use Latin alphabet letters.

But what to call it still isn't clear-cut. Most languages have their own version: Germans call it spider monkey; Danish, Norwegian and Swedish alternate between calling it pig's tail or elephant trunk. Finns call it cat's tail and in Hungarian it's worm. In Israel it's called strudel; French, Italians and Koreans call it a snail and in Czeckoslovakia it's a word meaning rolled-up herring.

So there are no rules, and no one word that supplies a name. English has turned out to be the most colourless — no elephants or rolled herrings or curly-tailed monkeys. In English it is just called 'commercial at'.

Q What does the 'new' expression *action figures* actually mean?

It means dolls for boys.

 Q When did *aerobics* begin?

Exercising to music (basically what aerobics is) has been going on for centuries. The activity is the descendant of what used to be called PT (physical training) or sometimes PE (physical exercise). Once upon a time it was called eurythmics but although the activity itself was not dissimilar, that name seems to have been discarded because it had an overly feminine image. (And eurythmics somehow doesn't sound as if the participants had endorphin highs.)

The word aerobics was first published in 1968 in a book by Kenneth Cooper, a former US military flight surgeon, who 'created' the fitness regime — and the name to go with it. The word is made up from the Greek *aer* meaning air, plus Greek *bios*, meaning life. Together they give the clue to what makes aerobics slightly different from all the other exercise forms — the process aims to increase oxygen in the blood. The routines are not static: you have to keep moving (and to be fashionable, give out falsetto 'yips' as well).

The associated terms jazzergetics, stretchomatics and limbercize, all mean much the same.

 Q Do *Afghan biscuits*, *Afghan rugs* and *Afghan hounds* originate in Afghanistan?

Afghan biscuits don't; they appear to be known only within New Zealand and appear to have got their name simply because they were dark in colour. They've been in the *Edmonds Cookery Book* since 1955. Nor does there seem to be any connection with the Afghani camel drivers who worked in Australia between 1860 and the 1920s, whose presence was responsible for the name The Ghan — the Afghan camel trains which took supplies to Alice Springs. But there's nothing known to link them with the brown New Zealand biscuits.

Shawls and rugs called afghans? Well, yes and no. We're into toponymy here — the naming of things after places: bikinis, denim, currants, tangerines, meringue, tweed, jodhpurs, spaghetti bolognese. (Note, though, that turkeys don't come from Turkey and guinea pigs don't come from Guinea!)

Shawls and knee-rugs have been woven in Asia for centuries. The word shawl comes from the Persian language but for many years the most desirable shawls were made in Kashmir. But then came the Afghan domination of Kashmir and by the 18th century styles and techniques were being copied and shawls called Kashmiri may actually have been made somewhere else. During the 19th century hundreds of shawls and rugs were being brought into Britain and by 1833 the term afghan was being used to describe a lightweight shawl for the shoulders — though it may not have come from Afghanistan, just from somewhere in Asia. By 1877 larger items described as knee-rugs were in use and these too were called afghans. The most recent development in this fashion is a rug-type shawl called a pashmina. This is a Persian word for woven goat's wool, but the shawls themselves are often made in Nepal. So we can say only that afghan shawls and afghan knee-rugs sometimes came from Afghanistan, but were sometimes more likely to have been made in the style of Afghanistan design (as often rugs advertised as 'Persian' may have been woven in Pakistan, but in a Persian style). Toponymy can sometimes be vague.

Afghan hounds actually originated in Egypt but the breed was developed and became famous in Afghanistan.

Q **Please explain the expression *all of a hoo*.**

It usually means that a person is discomforted but unable to pinpoint the exact area of discomfort. It is a contraction of all of a hoo-hah, meaning haphazard, chaotic and disorganised. The expression is thought to be derived from the French *brouhaha*. There is quite a collection of such sayings — feeling any old how, or all anyhow, or all of a tiswas or all of a doodah. Those last two do have an origin. Tiswas was an airmen's saying, meaning someone was getting overexcited; it's a development from hysterical. Doodah, too, was a flying term, referring to someone becoming nervous in mid-air.

Within the same family of expressions is out of sorts, which arose among old-time printers when sorts was the name given to particular pieces of type. If a printer had used up all the pieces of that type, he was out of sorts and naturally became a bit grumpy and distracted as a result.

Nowadays all of a hoo remains a non-specific, semi-nonsense phrase which indicates that a person is not at their best but can't give a specific reason.

Note also that the phrase all of a hoo-hah is French in origin and has no connection with the Maori word hoha, meaning unmotivated, a nuisance, boring.

Q What does *alpha state* mean?

According to the *Penguin Dictionary of Psychology*, it's the state of consciousness when the electrical activity of the brain sinks to between 8 and 12 hertz (waves per second). Thus it is a condition of deep relaxation.

When the brain is relaxed in its alpha state, it's the time for intuition, healing and emotions which defy scientific analysis.

There are various circumstances by which one can enter the alpha state: by being absolutely relaxed; the repetition of mantras; the use of hypnosis or self-hypnosis; the calm feeling associated with yoga; certain types of music that fit the natural rhythm of the heartbeat; and some stages of actually being asleep.

The beta state is a different situation, when the brain's activity changes to a rhythm between 17 and 25 hertz, which is a sign that the brain is involved in analysis.

What exactly is *Angostura bitters*?

It is a concoction made with the dried root of the gentian plant to which various vegetable juices and spices are added. The result is an intriguingly bitter, reddish-brown mixture intended to be added to cocktails and also to soups, salad dressings, gravies and even some desserts. A few drops in gin makes it go pink. The particular Angostura mixture was invented by a German doctor in Venezuela in 1824 and has been on sale around the world since 1830. There is a South American tree called the angostura which has a bitter bark, but the makers of Angostura bitters (J. Siegert & Sons of Trinidad) are adamant that the bark is *not* part of their mixture, which is named after the city of Angostura where the mixture originated. (It is slightly confusing in that the tree is still around but the city isn't. In 1846 the city of Angostura had its name changed to Ciudad Bolivar.)

Q **Is there a difference between *Armageddon* and *apocalypse*?**

In formal terms they are slightly different, although both words are sometimes used rather loosely to describe the end of the world as we know it.

Armageddon, a real place mentioned several times in the Bible, is Megiddo in Israel, said to be where the last armed conflict in human history will take place on the Day of Judgement. In the English language, the name Megiddo is usually said as Armageddon and has broadened in use to mean the scene of a large-scale decisive conflict, and sometimes the battle itself.

Apocalypse is also biblical and strictly means the vision of a prophecy, especially a violent or climactic event. That strict meaning has now been extended to refer to the actual disastrous events themselves.

In contemporary times, dictionaries acknowledge the change in use, and Armageddon and apocalypse are now used almost interchangeably, to refer to a cataclysmic event.

Why is a big plate sometimes called an *ashet*?

Ashet is an adaptation of the French word *assiette*, which has several meanings, mostly to do with being a base or foundation, so the word can be used to mean a course of a meal, or a platter on which a large amount of food can be placed. English, particularly Scottish English, modified the word to ashet. It usually means a big plate for holding meat, often with grooves along the bottom into which the juices drip. Like everything else, food is subject to changes in fashion, and it's not all that common now to serve huge amounts of meat from a big ceramic platter, but if this does happen you can refer to it as an ashet.

 Why does *at the drop of a hat* mean abruptly and without preamble?

The expression dates back to early America when fighting occurred and races were run without modern formalities or equipment. The beginning of a fight was signalled by someone throwing down or dropping a hat (it's mentioned in Mark Twain's *Life on the Mississippi*), and waving a hat downwards was a common signal for starting a race. Nowadays the phrase indicates that something happens without delay, without any fuss and with very little warning.

 Why do some people refer to *autumn* as fall?

The word fall, which is used in the United States, refers to the fact that, before winter sets in, the leaves fall off deciduous trees, leaving a stark landscape. The term hasn't caught on in New Zealand and doesn't really apply here because most of the native landscape is evergreen.

**When musicians talk about their *axe*
what do they mean?**

In general they mean the particular instrument they play and
probably carry round with them. The term axe is believed to have
originally referred only to saxophones — partly because their shape
is remotely like an axe, and partly because the two words axe and
sax have a similar sound.

B

How is it that women graduates — even married women — receive a degree called *bachelor*?

Bachelor is an ancient word that arose centuries ago from the Greek *bacca laureus*, referring to the berries of the laurel tree. The term has always been connected with a junior position in various hierarchies. Medieval young men who travelled in the service of a knight were known as bachelors and they aspired to become knights themselves. Their position survives today in one of the lower orders of knighthood — Knight Bachelor. In the days of the powerful guilds or early trade unions, a bachelor was a yeoman member of a trade guild.

Gradually the word drifted into two separate strands of popular meaning:

1. a man who isn't married, thus somehow giving him the connotation of being like the knight's assistant and the junior yeoman — a person who is unfinished, not fully qualified in life

2. a university qualification called a bachelor degree, which again is rather junior on the hierarchy scale, indicating the beginning of the climb towards higher academic levels.

All this development and usage took place over hundreds of years, long before there was the faintest idea of women going to university. The terms bachelor and master were well established as names of university degrees before women ever entered the system. By the time they did so, there was a word for a woman who wasn't married — spinster — but the women didn't want to be identified as Spinsters of Arts or Spinsters of Science. So the word bachelor remains as a degree title.

Was *Bali Hai* a real place?

The idyllic place is first mentioned in James Michener's 1947 book *Tales of the South Pacific*. The stories take place in the Solomon Islands in the Western Pacific. There is no place in the Solomons actually called Bali Hai but the locals point to a remote spot called Bala'la'e as the placename that inspired Michener. In 1949 the Rodgers and Hammerstein musical version, *South Pacific*, moved the entire action from Micronesia much further east into more picturesque Polynesia. By the time the movie was made in 1958 the entire setting of Michener's original stories was a distant memory. Filmed sequences supposedly taking place in Bali Hai were actually filmed on Santa Monica Boulevard in Los Angeles. Several places in the Pacific claim to be the real or original Bali Hai, but, alas, there's no such place and, if there were, it would be somewhere near Honiara in the Solomon Islands.

 How do we get the word *bamboozled*?

The word, which means to confuse, cheat, or mislead, goes way back to ancient Greece, where *bombyx* was the word for silkworm and from that developed the French word *bombace* and eventually the English bombast, describing a kind of light fabric. Because it was mainly used for padding, it was not considered valuable, and so the practice arose of using the word bombast to refer to high-sounding, inflated speech — words that were only 'padding'.

Somewhere round about 1700, the word bombast became extended into bumbazzle, meaning to play tricks with words and to confuse people with elaborate speech. This developed into bamboozle.

Q Why are tired feet referred to as *barking dogs*?

Cockney rhyming slang habitually drops off the word which actually rhymes and uses only the preceding word. So Barnet fair (hair) becomes just Barnet; loaf of bread (head) becomes just loaf; and daisy roots (boots) are just daisies. In this tradition, feet are sometimes called plates of meat, and sometimes called dogs' meat. And dogs' meat is, of course, shortened to dogs. So if feet are quite commonly referred to as dogs, it's a natural development that when they're worn out and tired, the dogs are in distress — they're barking. If your feet are sore and in pain, then your dogs are biting.

Q Does *beat around the bush* have anything to do with an actual bush?

Yes. It has come to mean proceeding deviously and not being direct. The beat originated with beaters, who travelled with game hunters and literally beat the bushes in order to flush out birds or other wildlife. If a person spent too much time beating a bush in a roundabout way, the prize game they were looking for might get away and be shot by some other hunter. So the term came to mean travelling a long way round, and from there it has extended to refer to long-winded speaking about something that could be revealed quite briefly.

Q From what language does the flower name *begonia* come?

None really, since it was a made-up word to commemorate Michel Begon, a French government officer sent on a naval mission to Santo Domingo in 1681. He brought back to Europe the first plant of the species that was later named after him — begonia.

Q **Is there confusion about the meaning of**
begs the question?

Yes. The misuse often occurs among people who are trying to sound grander and more sophisticated than they actually are. The expression dates back to the Latin *petitio principii*, where someone stacks the cards in an argument by assuming something that hasn't been proven before the argument begins. Begging the question is an attempt to persuade by using material that assumes that the speaker's own suppositions are correct.

Example: Does God exist? Answer: The Bible is divinely inspired so what the Bible says must be true, and the Bible says that God exists. Therefore, God does exist. That answer is begging the question: it uses the phrase 'divinely inspired' as part of its explanation, thus assuming that there is a divinity.

Misuse of the phrase can happen in the following manner, exemplified by a fictional news item: 'The government has announced that all secondary schools are going to be supplied with new computer equipment during the first half of 2004. This begs the question of where the money is going to be found so quickly.'

This use is absolutely, totally, 100 per cent wrong. The government's announcement *raises* the question of where the money is to come from. It does not beg the question at all. If in doubt, don't use the expression.

 Q **Exactly where is *behind the eight ball?***

It means that someone is in a potentially losing position. The expression comes from a pool game, where the black ball is numbered eight. If your move is positioned behind the eight ball, then you have a major problem. Being behind the eight ball is like being on the back foot.

What exactly is the difference between
better **and** *best*?

In English the descriptive function has three forms: positive, comparative and superlative. For example, one thing is good, another thing is better than the first one, and a third thing is the best of all three. If there are only two then you can't have a best, only the better.

Over the years this rule has caused various problems. For instance, the saying 'Put your best foot forward' should really be 'Put your *better* foot forward' because we have only two feet, not three.

For many years the New Zealand Broadcasting Corporation would not allow any superlatives in advertising so advertisers invented descriptions: soap powder washed whiter than white (because they weren't allowed to say whitest) and peas were fresher than fresh. This policy struck a big rock when an airline which had been proved by the aeronautical industry to be the world's largest was not allowed to say so on radio and television in New Zealand. So they pulled all their commercials saying 'We won't pay for advertising which does not allow a factual statement.'

 Who originally said *Better the devil you know*
than the devil you don't know?

The ancestor of the expression appears to be the words of the Dutch scholar Desiderius Erasmus, who said 'An evil thing is known best'. Later in the 16th century the phrase had become 'You had better keep those whom you know, though with some faults, than take those whom you know not, perchance with more faults.'

At some point over the following 300 years the concept of bad things or evil was replaced with the word devil and by 1857 Anthony Trollope in *Barchester Towers* used exactly the version we've become more familiar with: 'Better the devil you know than the devil you don't know.'

When you say *beyond the pale* are you referring to a real place?

It means outside the bounds of propriety or good taste or good sense and, yes, it does refer to a specific place. In this context, the word pale comes from the Latin word *palus*, meaning a wooden stake, which survives in modern English as the paling in a fence.

During the 14th century, the part of Ireland under English rule was marked out with a boundary of wooden stakes, and the boundary line was known as the English Pale. If Englishmen crossed over that line into Irish territory, they were leaving behind all the familiarities and niceties of English custom and rule — they were beyond the pale. This meaning became rather exaggerated, implying that you were leaving security and safety and going into the unknown. Gradually the expression settled down to mean outside the bounds of normal thought. By 1654 it had become a general expression — an archbishop of the Church of England wrote, 'No salvation to be expected outside the pale of the church.'

Q What is the history of the chime known as *Big Ben*?

First we should clarify that Big Ben was originally not the name of the famous clock in the British Houses of Parliament, but the name of the bell inside which sounded the hours.

The bell of Big Ben has been ringing since 1859. It strikes 156 times a day. There are four other bells, which strike the 'chimes', so in total there are 960 strikes a day. Strictly speaking, Big Ben does not strike chimes at all, just the hours, but over the years the meaning of the name has widened so that Big Ben is now generally used for the whole clock, all the bells and even the tower.

Big Ben is set to ring on the note E natural, the same as the big bell at St Peter's in Rome. The tune of the chimes that come before the hour originated in Cambridge, where a new clock was installed in 1793 and the Reverend Joseph Jowett was asked to compose a chime. He is believed to have been helped by one of his students, and between them they came up with the distinctive Cambridge chime, which was based on a fragment from Handel's *Messiah*: 'I Know that My Redeemer Liveth'. That chime was copied for the bells of the London clock and is now better known as the Westminster chime. It is often found in domestic grandfather clocks.

 What does the *big kahuna* mean?

The word *kahuna* is native Hawaiian and has been used there for centuries. The easiest way to translate it is to say that it's Hawaiian for wizard — not in the Harry Potter sense of pointy hats and magic spells, but more like a high councillor or expert with particular powers in the field of nature science. It could be described as close to the Maori word *tohunga*. It's rather like we would use the Hindi word *guru* — a spiritual leader and guide.

In recent decades kahuna has drifted into occasional use in English, sometimes in doubtful taste, because the word's real meaning has connotations that don't quite fit into contemporary English. It is distinctly disrespectful to translate the big kahuna as the big cheese, though this occasionally happens.

Are there reasons why some *biscuits* have exotic names such as Monte Carlo, Nice, Marie and Garibaldi?

Monte Carlo biscuits made by Arnotts have been on the New Zealand market since 1926. They're made with honey and coconut and layers of vanilla cream and raspberry jam. There's no available evidence that they were ever actually made in Monte Carlo, which is the main city of the tiny European country of Monaco. Their name appears to be simply a fancied link between the rather luxurious recipe and the luxurious image of Monte Carlo.

Nice biscuits are small, rectangular and frilly edged. They're named after the town in France and that's all anyone knows.

Marie biscuits are British and have been around, with that name, since at least 1870. Their name is very widely known in most countries with a British connection and they've been available in New Zealand since 1922. Marie biscuits are categorised as tea biscuits, meaning they're not very sweet and not very hard. They are similar to what in New Zealand are called Round Wine biscuits. Nobody knows definitely who Marie was, or why the biscuits bear her name.

Garibaldi biscuits actually do have a connection with Giuseppe Garibaldi, known as the unifier of Italy. This process included storming the island of Sicily. After Garibaldi's triumphant entry into Palermo, he took a liking to a pastry shop called Antica Focacceria San Francesco which made a special kind of bun filled with cooked beef spleen. (Don't panic, spleen is often eaten. It features frequently in Jewish cooking with the name *milts*.) The same shop in Palermo still serves these, and other buns filled with boiled bull's lungs.

This delicacy was not to everyone's taste, but the idea grew that Garibaldi liked munchies with a dark-coloured textured middle. This image somehow transferred Garibaldi's name to biscuits with dark-coloured currants, raisins and figs in the middle. (Such biscuits are also found in Palermo.) They're roughly what New Zealanders call fly cemeteries.

 Blenheim **in the South Island sounds like a German name. Is it?**

Yes. It's one of the few New Zealand places named after a place in Continental Europe.

In 1704 an early Duke of Marlborough, together with Prince Eugene of Savoy, routed the French and the Bavarians in the small German town of Blindheim. The battle was regarded as a brilliant British military victory. The Duke of Marlborough named his English home Blenheim Palace after the town of his great victory, but with an 'English' spelling.

More than a century later, settlers were arriving at the little place at the top of the South Island of New Zealand. The area became known as Beaver-town because the surveyors and the first arrivals had to live in trees and stumps to avoid the floods. Eventually the province was named in honour of the Duke of Marlborough's home and in 1860 Beaver-town was renamed Blenheim.

 Does *blimey* actually mean anything?

It's a shortened version of an oath meant to express surprise or disbelief. The original full version is God blind me, as in 'I'm so surprised at what you've just said that it's as if God suddenly struck me blind.'

Over the years it modified to gor blimey (gor being an abbreviation for God) and sometimes cor blimey. This is still further abbreviated to blimey or cor.

On *Coronation Street* Hilda Ogden once memorably looked up at an enormous oil painting of a huge battle scene and said, 'Cor, must 'ave 'ad a lot of numbers.'

 Where does the word *blog* come from and what does it mean?

It is a contraction of web log, which describes a certain kind of material that appears on the Internet, namely: a single column of chronological text, often updated, and usually written by one person, who is a non-professional writer. This means a diary, written on the Internet instead of in a book.

 There appear to be many expressions based around the word *blue*. Please explain some of them.

Blue for a boy: For many centuries — and for obvious reasons — the colour blue has been linked with the sky, and therefore heaven.

This gave the colour a connotation of superiority. Some cultures regarded male babies as more important than females, so the colour blue was associated with boy babies because it was a colour for superior people (meaning males!). On the other hand, because warmth and gentleness seemed to be associated with pink, girl babies were assigned that colour.

Blue moon: Some people think that under very special conditions — when there's forest-fire dust high in the air, or clouds of ice crystals, or after a huge eruption — the moon takes on a blue colour. It has been said that New Zealand had a moon that looked blue one night during 1922.

A belief also grew that when two full moons occurred in a calendar month, then the second of those was called a blue moon. But this isn't all that unusual: it happens about every three years.

The first known mention of blue moon can be found in the year 1528, but in a sardonic way, referring to something that's never going to happen. The implication is that a blue moon is a ridiculous impossibility. And that seems to be the most likely explanation for the way the phrase is used nowadays. It's rather like mentioning a moon made of green cheese or the twelfth of never.

Blue blood: Aristocrats don't really have this. The expression originated in Spain as *sangre azul*, which means exactly the same thing — blue blood. In centuries past, some areas of Spain were home to many people of Arabic or Moroccan descent, and racial mixtures produced families whose skin was darker than that of people of pure Spanish blood. Along with that, there was a resistance from rich people, especially indolent rich people, ever to expose themselves to the harsh summer sun. Spain is very hot in summer and those who had to work outdoors to keep themselves fed and housed, grew very swarthy. Grandiose people didn't like this look, and went to a great deal of trouble to keep themselves out of the sun and keep their skin as pale as possible.

On many people the blood vessels show a blueish colour through the skin. But if the person has someone of a dark race in their ancestry, or if they've been working on a farm or delivering mail in the city, then their skin colour precludes that blueness showing. Hence, only those people rich enough not to have to work in the sun, and of an ancestry that excluded anyone Arab or Moroccan, had blood vessels that showed as blue. So the description blue blood arose in Europe to describe people of unmixed European ancestry. Now we use the expression to mean those of aristocratic descent.

To scream blue murder: The expression arises from a double corruption. It began as a French expression, *mort Dieu*, the death of God, which was an exclamation of horror and shock, not necessarily involving a murder. Gradually the French corrupted that into a slang version, *mor bleu*, which crept into English as blue murder.

Blue-eyed boy: This expression was based on the belief that a person with genuinely blue eyes was fairly uncommon and usually attractive. So the person with blue eyes was often favoured by authorities. For much the same reason, a similar alternative was white-haired boy.

Bluebird of happiness: This concept was invented by the writer Count Maurice Maeterlinck, who in 1908 wrote a play about a boy and a girl who were seeking a visionary bluebird which represented happiness. (Birds that are a beautiful blue do exist, but they're rare.)

In 1934 Sandor Harmati, Edward Heyman and Harry Parr Davies composed the song 'Bluebird of Happiness'. The famous tenor Jan Peerce sang it in 1936 and his subsequent recording of the song probably did the most to make the concept of a bluebird of happiness very famous indeed. In 1940 Maeterlinck's original play was made into a movie, *The Blue Bird*, starring Shirley Temple. The film was remade, under the same title, starring Elizabeth Taylor, Jane Fonda and Ava Gardner. Curiously, though, Peerce's recording seemed to affect more people than the screen versions.

Blue as a nickname for red-haired men: This is somewhat mysterious. The habit comes from Australia and has been in use since the 1890s. Only one explanation seems to be on offer and although it doesn't have a solid provenance, it does seem to make sense. Making a blue is believed to refer to being in trouble with the law — summonses to court were issued on blue paper. And because red-haired men were believed to be hot-tempered, it was also believed that they got into lots of blues — problems and fights.

Blue movies: Blue may be the colour of heaven and of superiority, but it's also the colour of dirty jokes and pornographic movies.

Associating the colour blue with sexual activity comes from several sources. There was a Chinese custom of painting the outside of brothels a bright blue and the association of that colour carried over into Western culture to describe sex movies and jokes. But there's also a Christian image that associates the devil with burning brimstone — another word for sulphur, which burns with a blue flame. Hence in some circumstances the colour blue is associated with being bad.

There's also a third contributing factor. For many generations sub-editors in newspapers used blue pencils to make text corrections or to cut out material — either because it exceeded the space available or because it could be seen as offensive. Hence the term blue-pencil began to mean eliminate. And the term also led to an association with jokes or remarks that weren't suitable for publication and were therefore blue jokes because they'd been blue-pencilled.

The blues: As mentioned, the image of the devil was associated with the blue flame of brimstone/sulphur. This is also connected with describing unhappy people, who during the 1700s were said to be having the blue devils. They were depressed and dejected, so the devil must be getting at them with his blue fire. Gradually the term became just the blues. (A fanciful variation was found in Truman Capote's *Breakfast at Tiffany's* where Holly Golightly suffered occasional 'mean reds'.)

Music called the blues: Originally this was American music expressing the unhappiness of black people in the southern states. The music uses flattened notes on the third, the fifth or the seventh of the scale, which gives a sound falling between major and minor pitch. To ears accustomed to the diatonic scale, this sounds sad and carries a distinct connotation of melancholy.

Blueprint: This photographic process, invented in 1842, reproduced draughtsmen's and engineers' plans as white lines on a dark blue background. The meaning has extended to refer to a plan or project or a copy — not necessarily on paper — that other people can follow.

Blue ribbon: This goes back to the concept of the colour blue representing superiority. Knights of the Garter, the highest British order of publicly recognised achievement, began in 1348. Their insignia is a blue velvet band and a blue velvet cloak. The theme is often echoed at A&P shows and cooking contests, where the blue ribbon indicates the best level, the highest attainment or No. 1.

Cordon bleu: In medieval France, high-ranking knights wore medallions of rank hanging on blue silk bands. When they met, they wore their medals on the blue ribbon, and they were fed magnificent meals. Gradually the name of the ribbon on which the medal hung shifted to the splendour of the cooking.

Blue chips: In the gambling industry blue chips have the highest value. This has become a descriptive term for non-gambling entities which are considered reliable and valuable, such as a blue chip company or blue chip shares.

Q **What does *BMW* stand for?**

The letters stand for *Bayerische Motoren Werke* (Bavarian Motor Factory). In 1916 two aircraft manufacturers in the Bavarian area of Germany merged to become BMW. Their work was halted when the 1919 Treaty of Versailles forbade further manufacture of aircraft in Germany, so BMW moved on to motor cycles and railway parts. The company's first car was manufactured in 1928.

 Was *Bobby Dazzler* a real person?

No, there never was an actual person. Bobby dazzler is a British expression. The word dazzle came into English in the 1400s from an old Scandinavian word meaning to confuse, bewilder and confound. This meaning remains — if you get hit over the head you are dazed. But a secondary meaning also developed: dazzled, which referred to something which bewildered only the eyes. (Although the words have the same ancestor, if you're dazzled by a bright light it's slightly different from being dazed.) By 1800, the word dazzled had shifted to include things that weren't actually bright lights, but filled your eyesight metaphorically. So anything or anyone who was particularly attractive was a dazzler.

The word bobby is an odd one. Used in the north of England in the 18th century, it had a connotation of being in good health and good humour. Later on it developed an image of being small and neat, as in bobby socks and bobby pin. But in the 1800s when bobby was combined with dazzler it became an intensifier. Anyone who was in sparkling good health and good humour, and was good-looking, was a bobby dazzler. The term also extended to apply even to inanimate things. For example, a bobby dazzler was a particularly good marble!

 A newspaper cooking supplement refers to a *Bodum*. What is it?

A Bodum doesn't really exist as an ordinary word. It's the trade name for a kind of heatproof glass utensil, a plunger coffee-maker. When someone says or writes 'pour into a Bodum', they're using a trade name in the same way as we might refer to Vaseline or Ping Pong balls or Jandals, all of which are trade names.

Q   Is there a clear explanation for the word *bogan*?

This is one of those mysterious words. An exact definition is difficult because the word is extremely subjective. Anyone who says it will know what *they* mean by it, as will the people to whom they say it. But another group will have a slightly different understanding.

In general terms bogan is a contemptuous description applied to someone perceived as socially uncouth with a misguided fashion sense. The term is usually used in a downward direction on the socio-economic scale. It's remotely possible that an unkempt tramp could refer to someone on the Rich List or the Best-Dressed List as a bogan but it wouldn't really work.

Where does the word come from? Bogan originates in Australia and its public use began in 1988. Its actual origin is mysterious. The word exists in a real placename, the Bogan River in the Australian state of New South Wales. This is thought to be a possible source, because city people were inclined to refer to the area unkindly as a source of very strange, uncivilised country folk (in somewhat the same way as Aucklanders used to refer to the settlement of Puhoi, hence up the booai).

Whether the connection with the Bogan River is true or not, the word grew to become a pejorative for people whose clothes didn't please you. It developed connotations similar to words like nerd, dork and geek. Australia has various other words that can form a substitute for bogan: booners, boons, kevans, bevans — and, of course, westies, a term which originated in Sydney in the 1970s when people in the eastern suburbs regarded those in the western suburbs as socially disadvantaged. A westie is a moderately familiar term in New Zealand, particularly in Auckland, although cities without clearly defined east–west orientation tend to use the word bogan instead.

The big boost for bogan came in 1988 when a TV character called Kylie Mole performed weekly monologues that put several terms into the vernacular, such as spack (which didn't survive for very long) and bogan (which did). Mary-Anne Fahey, who wrote and performed the Kylie Mole scripts, said in various interviews that she caught the flavour of her monologues by listening to her 13-year-old daughter and her friends. So we might safely presume that bogan had been in use for a while before Kylie Mole made it commonplace in 1988.

Kylie Mole also clarified to whom the term could be applied, which turned out to be quite simple. Bogan described anyone she didn't like or didn't approve of; even something as minor as their socks could earn her stern criticism. Those criteria still apply, which is why the word is difficult to define but useful.

 Where does the golf term *bogey* come from?

The word *bogy* is an old Scottish word meaning ghost or spirit, or even the Devil. Somewhat aided by the popularity of the song 'The Bogey Man' (1890), the word bogey came to be used in golf to mean that the devil or the bogey man was an imaginary opponent and the bogey was the ideal number of strokes he would use to reach the hole.

There was a bit of a change in 1898 when lighter rubber golf balls came into use and fewer strokes were required to reach the hole, so the word par came into use meaning the new notional number of strokes required. In the United States bogey came to mean one stroke over par.

Explanations about English words often say the words are *borrowed from another language*. Do other languages do this?

Yes, they all do. A large proportion of languages nowadays have a complex set of borrowings from other cultures. Sometimes in English the words were borrowed several hundred years ago, and may be versions of Arabic, as with coffee, Scottish like whisky, Japanese like tycoon, Dutch like yacht, or Turkish as in tulip.

And all those languages are borrowing words from other languages all the time. For example, the word bar is fairly universal.

It has travelled into English through Latin and French but the English version is widely used, even in places like Japan.

As the centuries have progressed, people have travelled and invented things and been intrigued by other nations' foods or cultures or plants, with the result that words have criss-crossed into other languages, often changing their meaning as they do so. A language which is being used is flexible and moulds itself to what people want to say at any given point. And modern communication techniques have made words of all kinds more accessible than they ever were before.

The medical and legal professions tend to base a great deal of their communication on the Latin language, for the simple reason that it's no longer used in everyday life and is therefore unaffected by changes in meaning or borrowings. So when accuracy is vital in stating a law or specifying a medicine, very often Latin is the safest.

Some people are uncomfortable with the word borrowed, which usually indicates that whatever is borrowed will be returned. One could say that a word in English is derived, copied, modified or cloned from, or originated in, the other language. Although these terms are accurate, they sound clumsy. Informally, borrow seems to be acceptable.

 Is *bosh* a real word?

It is in Turkey, where the word comes from. In Arabic *mâ-fîsh* means there's no such thing and this is often shortened to *mûsh*. Turks somehow changed the m into a b, and by the time the word appeared in English (1834) it had become bosh, meaning nonsense, useless, there's no such thing.

Is the origin of the expression *bottoms up* as obvious as it seems?

Yes. It is believed to have originated at sea (as hundreds of words and expressions do) and simply means raising your glass, then tipping it and emptying it into your mouth so that the bottom of the glass is pointing upwards.

 There appears to be growing confusion between *bought* **and** *brought*. **Is this true?**

Yes, although the distinction is very simple. Bought means to have paid money, to have purchased. Brought means to have caused movement from a distant place to the place where you are.

Fund-raising fairs are often called bring and buys. The apparent confusion could possibly be allayed if they were called brought and boughts.

 How did having one's *bread buttered on the right side* **become a common expression?**

It means being alert to one's own interests, knowing what to do in order to gain an advantage for yourself. The expression came into common use as a quote from Sir Walter Scott's novel *The Bride of Lammermoor* (1819) where one character speaking of another says, 'No man knows so well on which side his bread is buttered.'

 What has a *brown study* **to do with the colour brown?**

Very little — the connection is slight indeed. Being in a brown study means that you're concentrating entirely on what's going on inside your head so you don't notice the passing of time or anything else happening in the real world. Your eyes are open but you're not really seeing.

The origin of the expression is French. When people were lost in concentration it was usually thought that they were feeling sad, so it was referred to as *sombre rêverie* — sad thoughts. In French the word *brun*, meaning brown, also can mean gloomy, as does the word *sombre*. Some confusion arose when *sombre rêverie* drifted into English. The *sombre* became muddled with the *brun* and it's been called a brown study since 1800.

Q Does *budgerigar* mean anything?

In the native Australian language, to which the word belongs, it means pretty little parrot. Budgerigar is one of the few Aboriginal words in international usage. The budgie, native to the grasslands of Australia, is now the most popular cage bird in the world.

Q How did the expression *bum's rush* arise?

The term is American, dating to approximately 1920 and originally meant forcible ejection. Some people believe it simply indicates that when a person is thrown out of somewhere, the onlookers see only the rejected one's bum rapidly leaving the premises. But there's also a belief that the expression arose originally in bars. When disreputable people like tramps, known in the United States as bums, staggered in, badly dressed and probably smelling a bit, they were rapidly sent away. Hence anybody given the runaround or asked to leave was being treated as if they were a bum, so they were getting the bum's rush.

Q How is the word *bunny* connected with rabbits?

Bun is a very old British dialect word meaning a little round cake. In the 16th century it began to be used to refer to rabbits and squirrels, possibly because they were small, warm and roundish. By the 17th century the squirrels had drifted out of the picture and bunny remained as an affectionate term for rabbits. (Rabbits in Britain aren't as much of a nuisance as they are in New Zealand.)

Q American television shows sometimes refer to a *bus* boy. Is this term ever used in New Zealand?

The expression is seldom if ever used in New Zealand. In the United States it describes the person in a restaurant who clears away the dishes and cutlery after they have been used. The term comes from Latin. A large horse-drawn conveyance which held a lot of people was developed during the 19th century. The French called this a *voiture omnibus*, a French-plus-Latin combination meaning a vehicle that was for everyone, omnibus meaning everyone, everywhere. This was the beginning of urban mass transport.

In time, and especially in Britain, the *voiture* was dropped off, and the large vehicle became simply an omnibus, which became a common word to describe large-scale transport for people all going in the same direction. It became shortened to today's bus.

The same meaning of omnibus — everyone, all people — also drifted into the American restaurant trade and by 1888 there is evidence that it was being used to describe assistants who did everything in a restaurant that the waiters didn't do, including the clearing of tables. In big restaurants, waiters usually have responsibility for an area or a number of tables, but an omnibus boy or girl, in the original Latin meaning of the word, can go everywhere to everyone, wherever there's a need to take away dirty cups, plates or cutlery. The term bus boy first appeared in print in 1913 and has been very common in the United States ever since.

In general, New Zealand has neither the job nor the expression — waiters generally clear tables. You'll sometimes hear the term commie waiter, believed to be short for communal or common to all areas. But that person is really an assistant to the main waiters. An omnibus, or bus, just clears dirty dishes, but never actually serves.

Q Why is certain American underwear called *BVDs*?

BVD were the initials of an American firm, Bradley, Vorhees & Day, which made the underwear in the first part of the 20th century. The name was too long to say all the time, so the firm was referred to by its initials — BVD. In time the men's underwear they manufactured was also called BVDs and the term is still used in the United States.

Q Where does the word *cajun* come from?

The provinces of Canada located on the Atlantic Ocean are collectively known as Acadia. Settlers there had strong links with France and spoke French. After Canada came under the rule of Britain, many Acadians refused to swear allegiance to the king, and from 1750 onwards started to emigrate to the United States, seeking a new life around the Mississippi in Louisiana. When asked who they were, the Acadians' French accent caused some confusion: the reply sounded like 'Ah-kay-jun'. From this the word cajun developed, pertaining to these people, their language, their music and, most famously, their food.

Q In the song 'Twelve Days of Christmas' what is a *calling bird*?

It's a mistake. The song was first published in 1780 and in those days it said colly birds. The word colly means something related to coal, therefore blackened by coal dust. So a colly bird was a bird that looked as if it were covered in coal dust — in other words a blackbird. (Colly survives in collier and colliery.)

Sometime in the following 200 years, people forgot that name for blackbirds, so colly didn't make any sense. Therefore printers started putting in calling bird, which didn't make any sense either.

Where did the expression a *can of worms* arise?

Canada. The imagery is fairly straightforward. A fisher's little pot of bait with its lid on might look neat and attractive and harmless. But if you take the lid off, there are worms and maggots inside — not an attractive sight. The expression started out as open a can of worms during the 1950s in Canada. Within 20 years it was in general use in the United States, and then around the English-speaking world. It generally signifies the revealing of unpleasantness or difficulties that were previously concealed, and may have been better left alone.

 What is the background to the expression *carte blanche*?

It is French for white paper or blank sheet. The term is military in origin, referring to situations of unconditional surrender. When a foe was clearly defeated, he was required to put his signature on a blank piece of paper, knowing he would therefore have to agree to whatever terms the victors filled in at their leisure.

Nowadays the expression is used in a figurative sense only, meaning that a person with a job to do or a project in hand, has no restrictions and no budget limit.

 Why are people asked if the *cat has got their tongue*?

There are two explanations for this, but the evidence for both is very scant. One version dates back many centuries to an old Oriental customs in which a thief was punished by cutting off his hand — and a liar was punished by cutting out his tongue. The severed body parts were actually given to the ruler's cats! So in some cases, the cat really did have someone's tongue — and obviously that person was no longer able to speak.

The word cat doesn't always mean the domestic kind, however. It is also the nickname of a nasty kind of whip called a cat-o'-

nine-tails, which had a handle and a bunch of leather strips. Being whipped by the cat-o'-nine-tails was such a terrifying prospect that people who were even threatened with that punishment became too frightened to speak. Some scholars believe that the expression the cat has got their tongue describes someone who is frightened, because they might be whipped.

Q **What does *catch a break* mean?**

In an American context break is often a shortened form of breakthrough. You'll hear it as a lucky break or just a break, meaning an unexpected advantage, while a bad break is an unforeseen stroke of bad luck. To give someone a break is to allow them an opportunity, and catch a break could be explained as seizing a chance that's fleetingly available. The popularity of surfing during the 1960s brought all kinds of surfing terms into wide public use — catch a break was one. Surf language also includes beach breaks, reef breaks and shore breaks. You'll find catch a break in Bob Harvey's book, *Rolling Thunder*. Surfers use it about very precisely defined moments, but the basic meaning is to take an opportunity.

Q **What is a *catchword*?**

Back in the days of handwritten manuscripts, a catchword was the separate word printed right at the bottom of a page, after the main text finished. This let you know what the first word was going to be on the next page when you turned over. You could catch the word on the hoof, so to speak, and not lose the flow of the sentence while you were turning over. Gradually the catchword shifted to the top of the page and can be seen in dictionaries as a guide to which spellings appear on the page beneath.

In time catchword came also to mean a few other things, such as the last word of an actor's speech which the next actor would pick up on, to deliver his lines. It was like a cue.

Then catchword came to be used for any word that caught attention. The term is widely used in advertising and politics when public attention is attracted with a word, or a group of words known as a catchphrase.

 How can it be assumed that *cats have nine lives* when everything else has only one?

It's a myth, of course: cats don't have nine lives. But they're particularly good at surviving disasters with the one life they do have. Cats are small, lightweight, fast and flexible and have excellent balance. Everybody has always known that cats can survive falls which other animals couldn't survive, and they can escape very quickly from risky situations. This somehow engendered the idea that cats have more chances at life than other creatures.

Ancient Egyptians revered cats, not only because they regarded them as having god-like qualities, but also because they were practical beasts and killed rats. And the Egyptians noticed cats' ability to survive falls and accidents. Thus they reasoned that it had more lives than the usual one.

Ancient Egyptians were also keen on numerology and the number three had significance for them, as it still does to many cultures. Anything three times three was especially significant, so it was honouring the cats to declare that they possessed three times three lives — nine. This belief inevitably drifted out from Egypt — it was mentioned in Arabic and Indian fables in the 8th century — and eventually reached the English language.

Ancient Egyptians weren't the only people to find significance in certain numbers. Even in modern times, the figure nine is ubiquitous — nine holes of golf, a cat-o'-nine-tails, nine-pins for bowling, Deep Space Nine, months of pregnancy, Cloud Nine, nine major planets, the whole nine yards, dressed to the nines. So it's not surprising that the concept of nine lives has a ring to it.

Besides the athleticism of cats, and the various resonances of the figure nine, the belief that cats had nine lives got tangled up with the medieval European belief in witches, so that the myth grew that witch-women could change themselves into cats, a total of nine times. That superstition faded away, but the belief in the cat's nine lives remained. It found its way into print in a book called *Beware the Cat* written by William Baldwin in 1553 and it's mentioned in *Romeo and Juliet* (approx. 1596). From then on the myth of cats having nine lives has remained in the English language.

Q **How did the fashion *catwalk* get its name?**

Obviously there's a connection between a cat's ability to walk along a narrow strip with no side support, and fashion models parading on a raised ramp with no rail. But the word isn't new. It has been in use since at least the middle of the 19th century, or possibly earlier, when parts of sailing ships were known as catwalks and building sites used the term for high, narrow communication bridges.

The phrase started to move into more common use around 1910–20 inside dirigible aircraft. A horizontal ladder-type structure on which the crew could move inside the aircraft from one part to another was called a catwalk. Later the term moved to other aircraft and was used in the Second World War to describe the long plank which stretched between the cockpit and the tail inside bomber aircraft. All these applications were sometimes called cat's walk rather than catwalk, but the s was gone by the time the term started being used in theatre and fashion shows, from about 1950 onwards. During the 1960s the terms ramp and walkway were still being used to describe the long narrow platform on which fashion models walked, but by the 1970s catwalk seemed to have become the universal term.

Q Is there is any connection between
a *charwoman* and a *cup of char*?

None. It seems they should be related but they come from entirely different ancestries. A very old English word, *cerr*, meant small amounts of work. That developed into two modern words — chore, which is usually a domestic job, and char, which means much the same thing and is associated with a woman doing domestic jobs.

But char when it means tea is Chinese — *ch'a* — and was simply borrowed into English more or less intact.

There's a third player in the field — char meaning to burn and blacken. This has no relation to the others; it's a shortened form of charcoal.

Q What does the expression *Chatham House Rules* mean?

A building in London called Chatham House is the base for the Royal Institute of International Affairs. Confidential matters discussed within the building have given rise to the phrase Chatham House Rules. This is a restriction placed on information discussed: when you're told something under Chatham House Rules you can use the information but you must cover your tracks and not attribute the information to any particular person.

Another version is sometimes said of a meeting held under Chatham House Rules meaning that information discussed at the meeting stays in the room and the details must not be discussed outside.

Q Has a *cheapskate* anything to do with skating?

There are two theories about the origin of this term. One school of thought thinks it is related to the Scottish and English dialect word *blatherskite*, meaning a boastful person (New Zealand prefers the shortened version skite). But there's also an old word *skate* meaning a worn-out horse. Therefore a cheapskate was a horse which didn't cost much but also wasn't much use. This has developed into meaning a stingy person who orders a job that is done for a low cost, but shoddily.

Are the little sausages called *cheerios* legally protected?

The name is legally protected within New Zealand only, and only as the name for little red sausages. Anybody can make little red sausages, there's no law against that, but only little red sausages made by Huttons can be called cheerios in New Zealand. The name was invented by Colin Munro, the then New Zealand manager of Huttons Meat Co., and the name was registered and protected in 1933.

How recent is the expression a *chip off the old block*?

The concept dates back to 270 BC, when Theocritus wrote of 'a chip off the old flint' meaning one who produces a parent's characteristics (usually the father).

By the 1600s the image had transferred to wood. Sometimes heard as chip of the old block, the phrase — or something similar — can be found in a 1626 play called *Dick of Devonshire*: 'Your father used to come home to my mother, and why not I be a chippe of the same blocke, out of which you two were cutte?'

How does a person come to have a *chip on their shoulder*?

It means to have a grievance, to bear a grudge, to be convinced that you're somehow disadvantaged and that things are deliberately set against you.

The expression was first noted in the United States when, in 1830, a Long Island newspaper described a schoolyard practice whereby an aggressive boy would place a piece of wood on one shoulder and dare someone else to knock it away. This was the equivalent of throwing down the gauntlet. It is believed that aggressive American boys had learnt of the practice among aggressive frontier men. He who knocked the chip off did so at his peril. So chip on the shoulder became a widespread way of saying that someone was belligerent and always ready for a fight.

There's also an alternative belief about the expression: that it comes from the days of saw-pits, when logs were sawn by hand. One person sawed from a top position on the log and the other was placed underneath. The man sawing in the lower position would be showered with chips from the upper sawyer, which was annoying and uncomfortable. Complaining about this led to his irritation being described as caused by a chip on his shoulder.

 Is the word voice necessary in the term *male voice choir*?

Probably not. Choir normally means people singing, but it doesn't always mean that. The term can legitimately be used to describe a group of orchestral instruments all of the same type — for example a brass choir.

Over time the word has more frequently been used to describe a formal group of people who sing. Cathedrals traditionally have all-male choirs, where boys sing the musical lines of sopranos and altos, but these are not referred to as male voice choirs. Neither is a singing group of boys, all with unbroken voices. What is referred to as a male voice choir consists only of *adult* male voices — tenors, baritones and basses, with perhaps just a touch of counter-tenor.

When musicians talk about *chops* do they mean from a butcher's?

No. *Chops* is a down-to-earth replacement for *embouchure*, which is the formal word meaning the position and control of the muscles around the lips and mouth, crucial for playing brass and wind instruments. This has given rise to the legend that women enjoy being kissed by brass instrument players because they're notably powerful in the lips! Gradually chops, meaning the mouth and lips in particular, has moved to a wider area so musicians now say it to indicate musical skill in general.

 The word *claddy* seems to exist but doesn't appear in any dictionary?

Yes, it exists — it means the stalk of a flax plant. The word isn't frequently heard, and it probably won't be in a British or American dictionary, because its origin is Maori. Claddy is an English version of the Maori word *korari* — the tall, straight stalk that arises from the middle of a New Zealand flax plant.

 Does *cleave* mean to stick to or cut from?

Both. To cut something in half is to cleave it, possibly with a cleaver. Yet if you adhere to a form of thinking or religion, or a particular relationship, it will be said that you are cleaving to it — sticking through thick and thin.

It is one of several bizarre English words that mean the same as their opposite, e.g. inflammable and flammable, and chuffed.

Is there such a thing as *cloud nine*?

Yes. Cloud Nine is part of the meteorological terminology adopted by the American Weather Bureau. The first *International*

Cloud Atlas was published in 1896. The development of aviation during the First World War increased interest in and emphasis on cloud formation, and an updated atlas was published in 1932. After the Second World War, a major update was published in 1956. This described 10 identifiable types of cloud divided into 14 subspecies.

There is a subdivision into general varieties of cloud, based on their transparency and their geometrical arrangement. These are listed according to their height from the earth. Their depth is also taken into account — the distance from the base of the cloud to its top. There are also four principal classes recognised according to the kinds of air motions that produce clouds.

Within the cloud species category, number nine is classified as a cumulonimbus cloud, which is slightly unusual because it's the only cloud within the classification that can have a base almost right down on the earth's surface.

But the top of that kind of cloud can reach to 60,000 feet, which is as high as standard meteorological cloud measurements go. (The World Meteorological Organisation uses feet as its standard measurement, so this would be about 18,000 metres.)

So cloud nine does exist and can be very high indeed. When a person is very happy, they feel in an elevated state, hence the expression being on cloud nine.

(Incidentally, the radio signal abbreviation pilots use for cloud nine is CB or Charlie Bravo = cumulonimbus. But they sometimes use a casual version, and refer to CB as Charlie Brown.)

Q Is *clowder* a real word?

Yes indeed, it's the internationally recognised term used to describe a gathering of cats. But it's not a word you hear very often. This could be because it's a fairly rare occurrence. You can see a herd of cows or a flock of sheep any day of the week, but cats don't normally gather in large groups.

The background to the word clowder is very strange. It developed from two ancient words, *clot* and *clod*, which were more or less interchangeable and both meant a shapeless lump. Descendants of the two words are still around. Clot became applied to a shapeless lump which had gathered in liquid, like milk or blood. Clod referred to a shapeless lump of something solid, like soil.

But clod was also sometimes said as *clodder*, and it gradually developed an extra connotation: it was used to describe a shapeless disorganised mass or group that was accompanied by pandemonium and even noise.

By the late 19th century four distinctly different words had settled down:

(1) clot — a shapeless lump, usually associated with liquid
(2) clod — another shapeless lump, usually solid
(3) clutter — a disorganised collection of generally stationery objects
(4) clowder — an untidy assembly of objects that moved around and possibly even made a noise.

Thus, clowder is the perfect word to describe an assembly of cats.

Q **What kind of fishing is called *coarse fishing*?**

The term originated in Britain, where game fish, salmon and trout, could be fished in waters to which the gentry had access. All the other people were confined to being coarse anglers, fishing in fresh water for other species. In general, coarse fishers use bait rather than flies or lures, and the fishing takes place in lakes, ponds and rivers. There are various coarse fishing clubs around New Zealand and versions of the term are widely known and used in other countries. New Zealand coarse fish include rudd, perch, tench, carp and catfish.

Q **What are the *cockles* of your heart?**

In 1669 the English physician and physiologist Richard Lower wrote *Tractatus de Corde* (Treatise on the Heart) in which he referred to the ventricles of the heart as *cochlea cordis*, meaning shell-shaped. Arising from that Latin term, the casual version cockles seeped into English as meaning the very depths of the heart — both literal and figurative.

 How did an elderly man become a *codger*?

Nowadays, the word codger normally describes a slightly eccentric old person and is faintly affectionate. It becomes a criticism only when it has a couple of adjectives in front of it, e.g. a mean old codger, a drunken old codger.

The origin of the word dates back to the 1400s when Britain had a good many travelling salesmen attending village fairs and also going door to door. They were known as *cadgers* and had a slightly disreputable air.

Over the space of 200 years, the word *cadger* developed into two different words. One of those came to mean a person who borrowed stuff all the time, or was always looking to use someone else's advantage. That meaning remains today.

But *cadger* also slowly developed into codger, meaning an old person who was a little contemptible. Gradually the contempt died away from the word, and from the 1800s onwards calling someone a codger ceased to be a put-down. It simply means that they're old, and possibly a wee bit eccentric.

 Why do we say someone has been given the *cold shoulder*?

The expression was first seen in print in 1816 in Sir Walter Scott's novel *The Antiquary* when a countess turns her back on someone dismissively (Scott himself explained the meaning as 'cold and reserved'). Thus the expression appears to have begun as literal — showing disdain by actual body language. In later years it has extended to a figurative sense — to ignore, to be unwelcoming, to treat with hauteur.

A secondary explanation is sometimes offered. In medieval times, when house guests were staying, new meats were cooked for them every day and served hot. If the guests stayed too many days and became a nuisance, then the host would stop cooking new meals and would serve them the previous day's meat — often a shoulder of mutton — now cold and considered inferior. So the overstaying guests would get the message.

Q **Why are so many places called _Columbia_?**

A university, a country, a film studio, a district of Washington — most of the places and institutions named Columbia are named after Christopher Columbus. There was a Saint Columba in Ireland in 597 and an Italian theatre character called Colomba or Columbine, but neither of those made the same impact on the world as Christopher did. He seems to be the reason why we have so many Columbias.

Q **Why is the word _cool_ so cool?**

This must be one of the most difficult words to elucidate. Its meaning is usually quite clear to the person using it, and those hearing it, but it's hard to pin down what might be called a dictionary definition.

Cool in its modern sense of being self-possessed was not originally an American concept, but British. It dates back to 1857 where it can be found in the book _Duncange Anglicus_.

Certainly it was in the United States that the term gained wide popularity. Scott Fitzgerald used it in _The Great Gatsby_ (1925). During the 1930s cool was used among jazz musicians and jazz fans as a term of praise for new and pleasing jazz styles. It went quite quickly into general use in the United States and Canada, and since approximately 1945 has been used worldwide as a modified term of praise.

When a thing or a person is described as cool, it usually means self-possessed, aloof, disengaged. Hence the use of such expressions as a cool million which originally indicated that the person dealing with that amount of money was stoic and not showing naïve excitement. Such qualities aren't always required; particularly among the young cool simply designates something, anything, of which they approve. (For the reverse, see **bogan**.)

As a noun, cool tends to mean balance or control — to keep your cool, to lose your cool, or to remain cool. As a verb, to cool usually means to postpone or to lose interest — let's cool on the deal for a while.

Of course cool can also mean slightly chilly, but using it for that meaning isn't cool.

 The supermarkets now sell *corn syrup*. Is it really made from corn?

Not directly. Corn contains no syrup but the kernels do contain starch, which is made into cornflour. At a later stage, corn syrup is man-made by chemically processing the cornflour with acid treatments or enzyme treatments, which manipulate the cornflour's starch components into three kinds of sugar: glucose, dextrose and maltose. The result is a clear, intensely sweet syrup that can be described as 'natural' but only just.

(Golden syrup is entirely different: it's extracted from sugar cane and totally natural.)

 How did *cos lettuce* get its name?

From the Greek island of Kos where it comes from.

Is there a difference between *cost* and *price*?

Yes, there is a slight difference. Cost means that which is paid for acquiring something, usually measured in money. Price means the sum of money or goods for which anything may be bought or sold. Note that the word sum means the total amount required.

Price, being the total amount, can be made up of several smaller *costs*. An advertised cost can have the term 'plus GST', indicating that more money than the stated cost needs to be placed on the counter to meet the required price. The words became a matter of dispute in New Zealand when airlines began to advertise amounts which looked like prices but turned out to be only one of the costs: the small print mentioned other costs (insurance charge, domestic passenger levy, government security levy, phone booking fee) which eventually added up to a larger price than was immediately apparent.

If a person understands something, why do they say they *cotton on*?

It means to understand an idea that's being presented, or to like someone and become friendly with them. The saying is believed to have originated in cotton mills, where tiny bits of thread or cloth were inclined to stick all over whatever you were wearing and were a nuisance to pluck off. So cotton on gradually acquired this sense of adhering to something or someone. Eventually, when someone grasped the basis of an idea they were being told, it was as if the idea had stuck, and was being understood. Hence, they had cottoned on.

What is *a country mile*?

A country mile usually means a distance perceived as longer than an ordinary real mile. The term is so old that its origin can't be pinned down exactly, but it's believed to have arisen because people in country areas lived further apart than in urban areas. Thus country people were accustomed to travelling considerable distances to visit each other or transact business. A country person thought a journey of several miles was quite a quick trip, because it was a common occurrence. To urban people, such a distance was a slow, ponderous and bumpy country ride. So when urban folk said a country mile they were intending to convey that the distance was long and harder to endure than travelling an ordinary mile.

Nowadays, when we say something doesn't come within a country mile we are indicating that it missed by a very long way.

Q **Do cows actually have *cowlicks*?**

The term cowlick has been in print since at least 1825 although it isn't strictly accurate. The lock of hair that stands out over a human forehead does resemble the oddly shaped patch of hair on a cow who has been licking an itchy spot. But a cow sometimes has swirly patches of hair that look as if they've been licked, though they're in places the animal couldn't possibly reach. The patches can happen just as randomly on a cow as on a human head, even when neither has been licked.

Q **Why does the term a *cut above* indicate superiority?**

One of the meanings of cut is a grade, or quality. So if a person or a thing or an event is a cut above it is of a higher quality than something else.

Q   **How is the *date of Easter* sorted out?**

Jesus was Jewish, and the actual events with which Easter is concerned — the trial and death of Jesus — are reported to have happened while he was taking part in the Jewish celebration of Passover. That festival was celebrated for centuries before Jesus was born and is still celebrated all over the world. Passover dates are known to all Jewish people. Therefore it would be quite simple for the Easter festival to be held on exactly the anniversary date of Jesus's death. But Passover dates are calculated by a lunar calendar, not by the standard 12-month Christian calendar. Therefore Passover is on slightly different calendar dates each year. Christians went along with this for several hundred years but found it inconvenient.

Christian missionaries travelling through Europe to carry their story couldn't avoid noticing that because the time of Easter was roughly equivalent to the coming of spring, there were already a number of festivals in place to rejoice in the warmer weather. So, during the eighth century, it was decided that the observance dates of Easter would attach themselves to the long-established festival periods, and that Easter would become 'weekendised'. The festival would be symbolic and commemorative only, rather than being on the actual dates of Jesus's death (as Christmas is commemorative of Jesus's birth and is not on the actual date). To this effect a system was worked out whereby every year Easter Sunday would occur on the first Sunday following the first full moon after the (Northern Hemisphere) vernal equinox (or if the full moon after the equinox falls on a Sunday, then Easter Sunday will be a week later). Considering the original reason for the changing of the festival date, strangely the 'new' system still puts Easter on different dates each year (it can be from 22 March to 25 April), but at least with the convenience that it is always a weekend.

(See also **hot cross buns**, **Easter eggs**, **rabbits**, name of **Easter**)

 ### What is the origin of the names given to *days of the week*?

In English, the seven days of our week come variously from ancient Latin, ancient German and ancient Scandinavian. They just grew that way.

Monday is named after the moon. Tuesday comes from the word *Tiu*, the Norse word for one of the gods of war. He was a relative of Odin, another god of war, who was sometimes called *Woden*, thus giving us Wednesday. So Tuesday and Wednesday are both named after gods of war. Thursday is pretty noisy too — it's named after *Thor*, the Norse god of thunder. Venus was the goddess of love (you'll find her in the French name for this day — *vendredi*) but the Scandinavian version of Venus was a lady called *Freya*, and so the English language adopted the Scandinavian name rather than the Roman one, and so *Freya* became Friday. *Saturn* was the Roman god of seeds and harvest, who unfortunately ate nearly all his own children, but nevertheless Saturday is named after him. Everybody needs light and heat, so Sunday is named to commemorate the sun, source of light and heat.

 ### Some clarification, please, about *dead* certainty and *dead* giveaway.

Dead doesn't just mean absence of life, it has a secondary meaning of completely and thoroughly, as in dead drunk, dead beat, dead against, dead heat, dead accurate, dead certainty, dead right, dead broke, dead tired, dead stupid, etc. In that context the word dead becomes an intensifier, making whatever it's describing more intense.

How did anyone find out Jesus was born on 25 *December*?

They didn't. Nobody knows when Jesus was born. The date of 25 December is commemorative rather than being an accurate anniversary. So many existing pre-Christian festivals were held in Europe during December that in AD 350 Pope Julius I decided to attach the Christian celebration of Jesus's birth to the existing festivities, and 25 December was declared to be the date for celebrating Christ's Mass. But there is no definitive information about either the date or the year when Jesus was actually born.

 When referring to schools, news broadcasts talk about *deciles*. What exactly is a *decile*?

It is a method of placing things in an order or rank, from 1 to 10. In theory it could be used to describe anything, such as one of those talent quests where people hold up a card showing a number up to 10, to evaluate the performance. Or when we say among ourselves, 'On a scale of one to ten, how did you enjoy the party?'

In New Zealand decile is used as a way of describing the financial position of the district in which a school is situated, 1 being at the lowest socio-economic level, and 10 at the highest.

This ranking has absolutely nothing to do with the quality of the school, the integrity of its principal, the expertise of its staff or the potential success of its pupils. The decile number is allocated to each school by the Ministry of Education after it has studied the census information about that district, and decided what the level of wealth is in the surrounding population.

 Please clarify the differences between *desert*, *dessert* and *deserted*?

(1) Desert — a region almost devoid of vegetation, especially because of low rainfall (from the Latin *deserere*, to abandon).

54

(2) Desert — to leave without intending to return, to avoid responsibility (also from Latin *deserere*, to abandon).

(3) Desert — a reward or punishment which has been earned (from the French *deservir*, to be worthy of).

(4) Dessert — the sweet course of a meal, usually at the end (from French *des* + *servir*, to clear a table).

 Does the word *diaper* belong to babies or to mathematicians?

Both can claim it. The English word diaper comes from the ancient Greek *aspros* meaning white, which gives *dia-aspros* — through whiteness. During the 15th century the word was used to describe a type of white fabric characterised by being woven in a diamond pattern, with a little woven insignia inside each shape. Apparently some 200 years later, in the 17th century, the term diaper began to be applied to the geometric design on the fabric. The term's use then broadened to describe any geometric shapes that were repeated to fit into a prescribed space.

Far from geometric designs, in the United States the word is widely used to name something entirely different — a baby's nappy is a diaper, sometimes shortened to didy. (It's a great demonstration of faith that Americans call a baby's nappy by a name which means white.)

Clearly then, diaper means two quite different things. Diaper meaning a nappy is descended from the name of the centuries-old white cloth weave. And the cloth with its repeated pattern gave its name to a repeated pattern discipline of geometry.

 Disgruntled **is fairly common but you never hear its opposite, gruntled. Why?**

It is strange. You can *dis*mantle something and be *dis*gruntled, but you don't hear mention of anything mantled, or gruntled. It's true that dis means opposite, as in disgrace or disestablish, but it can also be just an additive to an existing word — there doesn't have to be an opposing prefix available to negate the dis.

There is a word mantled. You don't hear it often, but it does exist. If someone is mantled, they are wrapped in a cloak, covered, complete. If dismantled, they are uncovered and pulled apart.

Disgruntled isn't quite the same. Gruntled comes from the old English word *grunnettan*, which indicated a short, snuffling noise, rather like the snort of a pig. Pigs make this snuffling sort of noise when they're happy, so the word disgruntled developed the opposite meaning, calling to mind the noise pigs make when they're unhappy.

Gruntled isn't heard much, possibly because a happy pig is not found very often in an urban environment.

 A newspaper reported that a compere was *dissing* the sponsors. What is *dissing*?

It's a shortened version of showing disrespect. The term arose from hip-hop language, which is heavily influenced by Black-American vernacular.

 Does the term *distaff side* relate to spinning?

In contemporary times distaff is a perfectly respectable word meaning female. It isn't offensive and it isn't a put-down; it's simply a way of designating ancestry through the female line — the distaff side, or mentioning the proportion of women employed on a project, the distaff numbers.

The term does relate to spinning. The distaff is a staff around which flax fibre is placed, and the flax drawn from it is spun into thread. Historically this was always done by women and the word distaff came to mean women in general. So descent from the distaff side came to mean through the female line. (Another spinning term developed to describe the unmarried women who, without dependants, sat at their spinning wheels — spinsters.)

In genealogy, the male version of the distaff side of a family is correctly called the spear side, because only men carried spears.

Q | **Who wrote the line *'Distance lends enchantment'*?**

Many people believe it was William Wordsworth but no, it was the poet was Thomas Campbell (1777–1844) in *Pleasures of Hope*, written in 1820:
'Tis distance lends enchantment to the view,
And robes the mountain in its azure hue.
(see also **few and far between**)

Q | **Why are horses often referred to as *Dobbin*?**

The word dobbin is an old English childish version of Robin, which itself is a form of Robert. The dobbin version has been in use, attached to horses, since the 16th century. It was used to describe the wickerwork horse shape worn by people in carnivals — a dobby horse. Sometimes it was a fairly primitive wooden bar with a horse's head and tail, which children pretended to ride.

(This *dobby horse* eventually changed its pronunciation to hobby horse, and developed a new shade of meaning — namely, that when a person is rattling happily on about some topic that interests them you say they're on their hobby horse because they think that what they're saying is of interest to everyone, when it really isn't.)

During the 19th century, the dobbin word had a big boost. And a slight change came about regarding the kind of horses to which the word was applied. This change came, as language expressions sometimes do, from a work of fiction, William Makepeace Thackeray's *Vanity Fair*, which began to appear in serial form in January 1847. That book has a character called William Dobbin who is a figure of patience and long suffering, and the book became so well known that the existing horse word Dobbin drifted towards horses of a similar ilk to the character of William Dobbin: patient, amiable, slow-moving and kind-natured.

 Why is the highest level of university degree called a *doctorate*, sometimes a *doctor of philosophy*?

The word doctor arises from an ancient French word meaning to teach. Obviously the person who taught something had to have detailed knowledge of the subject being taught, so gradually the word doctor came to be used to describe someone with great knowledge. By the 13th century there was a firm connotation that someone called a doctor was very learned and so the word became attached to the highest degree in the university system.

As a side issue, because people with medical knowledge and expertise were the ones the public had most contact with, the custom developed of calling these people doctor even when they didn't hold a doctoral degree. This practice is still current, and the title doctor is used variously among dentists, vets, opticians and general practitioners of medicine.

Qualifying for a doctorate can happen in various ways, according to different universities' rules. One kind is awarded on the evidence of examination and practicalities, such as clinical work in the medical area. A doctorate of philosophy is sometimes slightly different because it is usually awarded on the result of a thesis (a formal and systematic examination of a key area within the subject being studied). A thesis is seen to be an intellectual exercise rather than a hands-on practical demonstration of knowledge and because philosophy means the love of learning, that degree is referred to as a Doctorate of Philosophy in whatever the subject is. The graduate has demonstrated intellectual fitness and a love of learning.

Why were battles between war planes called *dogfights*?

Dogs when they fight each other specialise in close combat. In the First World War when air combat involved planes fighting each other at close quarters, this quickly became dubbed a dog fight and the term seemed to stick.

 When someone is in disgrace, why are they in the *doghouse*?

The saying is believed to have originated with Peter Pan, the character created by Sir James Barrie in 1904. The Darling children were looked after by a motherly dog named Nana, to whom their father was less than kind. When the children disappeared (on a trip to Never-Never land) Mr Darling was so contrite that, to atone for his earlier ill temper, he moved into Nana's kennel and remained there in disgrace, until the children came back.

 Where did the names *doh*, *re*, *mi*, etc. come from?

Guido d'Arrezzo was an 11th-century Italian monk credited with organising the writing of musical notation into the ancestor of the system we use today. The original scale notes were named after the first words of each line of a Latin hymn:

Ut queant laxis
Resonare fibris
Mira gestorum
Famuli tuorum
Solve poluti
Labii reatum
Sancte **I**oannes.

In those days *Ut* was the first note and *Si* the seventh — contrived from the initial letters of the Latin for St John. At a later stage Italy changed the *Ut* into *Do* (as the first syllable of Dominus) and *Si* was replaced by *Te*, so that each scale note had a different alphabet letter representing it.

 How did we come to say a person in financial difficulty has *done in his dough*?

Done is the past tense of do, and one of its meanings is finished — the cake is done, the gardening is done, the job has been done. The expression done in generally means physically exhausted: after a sports match or a tiring day a person says, 'I'm done in' to mean that they're tired out, and can't do anything more. If a person's money has run out, is exhausted, finished, then it, too, is done in.

Our passion for abbreviation often causes the in to be left out, so you'll hear he's done his dough. That shorter version has a slightly different connotation of the person having lost money through foolishness or trickery, e.g. he won Lotto and developed a lavish lifestyle and now he's done his dough, or they put money into an Internet business scheme and they've done their dough. Sometimes the expression doesn't mean totally broke but just that the specific money referred to has been lost, never regained.

Q **What is the background to *draw a line in the sand*?**

A line drawn in the sand is totally unstable — any reference to sand immediately indicates something that shifts — but curiously, the expression is frequently heard in a sense indicating firm action, a final decision.

This is an example of one expression becoming confused with another. A line in the sand sounds silly if you're wanting to sound decisive but recently it has been used in that sense. Scholars and etymologists believe it to have arisen from confusion with another expression — to draw the line.

The two images have been confused for centuries. It is reported that in 168 BC, the ambassador of the Roman Senate demanded that King Antiochus withdraw his siege of Alexandria in Egypt. The ambassador drew a circular line in the sand around the king and ordered him to give an assurance of withdrawal before he stepped out of the circle. The king complied, and evacuated his army.

In 1530 the explorer Francisco Pizarro was ordered by the governor of Panama to stop his expedition to Colombia, but Pizarro defied the order and is reported to have drawn a line in the sand and asked those men who desired wealth and glory to step over the line and join him.

The newer and shorter expression to draw the line wasn't sighted until 1793. Its origin has never been clarified: either the new-fangled game of tennis which drew lines inside which the game took place, or a plough-line in farmland to demonstrate a farmer's territory.

Either way, the meaning has always been quite clear: a limit has been defined and a perimeter of acceptability has been laid down.

To muddy the issue further there's a common expression in the United States: to draw a line in the dirt, which was supposed to have begun at the 1836 Battle of the Alamo when the battle proved hopeless and a line was drawn in the dirt; those who stepped over it decided to give up and die. But that story has been discarded as not true.

There's also another American expression, line in the dirt, which denotes a boundary. In a children's playground a bossy child will draw a line and say, 'You're not allowed over that line.' And that line could be in the dirt — or in the sandpit.

Around 1970 these various meanings appeared to blur in the United States, especially among politicians (who often appear to prefer six words where three would do).

They began to say drawing a line in the sand, when they actually meant drawing the line or creating a firm limit. People who say they're in the know report that when the first President Bush spoke of a line in the sand when referring to Saddam Hussein, he intended to say *draw a line in the dirt* but changed the words because of the vast amounts of desert in the territory to which he was referring.

To be safe, best forget sand if you wish your statement to sound firm. Try less confusing expressions like engraved on tablets of stone or set in concrete.

Q How did the word *duffer* come into being?

It's a fairly common word, meaning a person who is foolish, clumsy or simple, but the origin isn't simple at all. Duffer appears to be related to two very old English words. At the end of the 1700s to duff meant to cheat someone or pass fake money. And there was another word with a rather indelicate sound — dowfart, which meant a slow-witted person.

Perhaps because of a growing concern over which words one could say publicly and which one couldn't, dowfart gradually softened into a version that sounded like duff but finished up as duffer.

(There is no connection between a duffer, a fool, and a duffel coat, which is named after the town of Duffel in Belgium.)

Q What does the word *duvet* actually mean?

There's a difference between how it has come to be used in English, and what it actually means. *Duvet* is French for down — the fluffy type, from birds. So we call the whole thing a duvet, assuming it is filled with down and soft feathers. The French call the same thing a *couette* and there are other English names: an eiderdown, a continental quilt, a comforter, a puff. Australians tend to say doona, which is the trade name for an Australian soft-filled-cover, based on a Scandinavian word for down.

Q There seems to be confusion about the word *dwang*?

There could be, if you don't make the territorial adjustment. The English word dwang is derived from a Dutch word meaning strength and it travelled into English through Scotland. From there on it has developed two entirely different uses. In large parts of British industry (such as Mersey shipyards) a dwang is a strong wrench used for turning taps and reamers.

But in New Zealand a dwang is a piece of timber secured horizontally between upright vertical studs, to strengthen a wall frame. The word has been used in that way since approximately 1900.

There is no clear explanation of how this has happened — the two uses of the word are entirely different, although both are concerned with strength.

In places where dwang does not mean a horizontal support for vertical studs, the word nog or noggin is used. A nog was originally a small brick-shaped piece of timber in a brick wall, placed at a point where a nail was required. When timber houses became more common, small pieces of wood were needed between studs on a weight-bearing wall. Because these resembled the nog used in brick houses, the word was transferred to the support piece for vertical studs.

Q What is *dystopia*?

An imaginary place. Back in 1516, Sir Thomas Moore dreamed up an image of a perfect society, living in a place he called Utopia (from the Greek for no place). Over 300 years later, British philosopher John Stuart Mill launched a cynical opposite version — Dystopia. This was the stark and unpleasant counter-image to a perfect society. The word is usually used now to refer to a fictional situation, where social trends being practised in the present go sour in the near-future. The theme frequently occurs in contemporary science fiction.

E

Q **What do golfers mean when they talk about an *eagle*?**

It will be no surprise that the term is related to another golf term, birdie. Because birds fly so expertly, the American expression birdie was applied to anything that appeared to be excellent. So in American golf, since the early 1900s, a birdie was reaching the hole in one stroke below par (the notional ideal). From that developed eagle, a grander version, meaning two strokes below par.

Q **Is the name of *Easter* anything to do with yeast?**

No. The name comes from festivals held in ancient times to celebrate Eostre, who was goddess of the dawn and the spring. When the Christian religion began to develop, it adapted existing festivals; in this case Eostre slowly became Easter.

Q **Does *eavesdropping* have anything to do with eaves?**

Once upon a time, it did. The little piece of roof that hangs over and beyond the outside walls is the eave. People used to believe that if you wanted to hear private conversations going on inside a house, then you should stand hard against the wall, as close as possible to the eaves because sounds would echo just there. So you could stand around underneath the eaves and if anybody saw you, you could pretend you were just dropping in to visit. Modern building materials and high-rise housing have made such clandestine activity impossible but when someone is listening when they shouldn't be, it's still called eavesdropping.

How did so many prominent places around Auckland gain the name *Eden*?

Like everyone else in the Western world, the aristocrats of Britain have a surname, though usually only their title is mentioned. For instance the Dukes of Bedford have the surname Russell on their passport and the Lords Cobham have the surname Lyttelton.

In the mid-19th century, the Earl of Auckland (First Lord of the Admiralty and ultimately Governor-General of India) was a friend of Governor Hobson. Lord Auckland was paid the compliment of having the New Zealand city of Auckland named after him.

But his actual surname was Eden. Hence the sprinkling of Eden names around the city: Mount Eden and the suburb surrounding it, including the sports stadium, Eden Park, and the botanical spread of Eden Gardens. Beautiful though they are, they have nothing to do with the biblical garden of Eden.

Q **Does anyone ever really have *egg on their face*?**

It means to come out of an experience badly, and to look foolish, usually because you have brought humiliation upon yourself through some massive lack of judgement. An exact starting point for the expression is not known, but some commentators believe it arose from American election campaigns in rougher days, when doubters would express their opinion of some candidates with a well-aimed egg. Another simple source is the image of someone who has eaten a runny boiled egg but has not wiped their face afterwards and is unaware that there is yolk running down their chin.

Egg on your face is not a very old expression. It came to light in the 1970s and was swept into worldwide use by Sir Freddie Laker who was widely quoted saying it when there was a dispute between British Airways and Laker about running Concorde at a profit. This often happens: that an existing expression becomes famous overnight.

Alison Holst includes a cautionary note in her book about microwave cooking. You must always prick an egg yolk before putting an egg into a microwave. With her usual straightforward pragmatism, Mrs Holst advises, 'If you forget to do this, you will only ever forget once.'

 What have *eggs* got to do with Easter?

Easter commemorates a death and celebrates a resurrection. Because the egg contains the potential for a new living creature it has been a symbol of birth and new life for centuries, even in non-Christian districts and philosophies. In the Northern Hemisphere it is associated with the season of spring. The egg's long-standing association with fertility and life was gradually taken over by Christians to give Easter a resonance as the celebration of a particular resurrection into a new life.

 What is the relationship between *eleemosynary* and *alms*?

They come from the same Greek root but they have arrived in English with different shapes. Both words travelled through medieval Latin and by the time they reached English one had become eleemosynary, which usually means a person who is poor and depends on charity assistance, and alms, which is the money or assistance given out.

These divisions from a common root happen frequently. You say a craftsman is restoring your broken china, and you also go to a restaurant. The two words sound different, are spelt differently and have different applications — but both stem from the word restore.

Q **Is it true that Sherlock Holmes never said** *'Elementary, my dear Watson'*?

Quite true, the phrase does not appear in any of Conan Doyle's books. Holmes sometimes said, 'Elementary' and sometimes said, 'My dear Watson', but never the two together. It is a misquotation that developed later.

Q **Where are you, when you're at the** *end of your tether*?

It's to be hoped you'll never be there, since the image is strictly from the animal kingdom. A tether is the rope or chain used to confine an animal to a certain area. This can become extremely frustrating. Therefore when someone is in a situation that is causing severe frustration and straining their endurance, they say they are at the end of their tether.

Q **Is it valid to say** *England and Europe*?

Absolutely not — England is a part of Europe. Occasionally you hear comment and even see travel brochures that have them as two separate things, but this is nonsense. Geographically, Europe is a mass of land and islands, each with a connection to the other by race, language, history and culture. Saying England and Europe is like saying Hawaii and the United States, or New Zealand and Stewart Island. A more accurate terminology is England and the Continent.

Some people are vague about distinctions, and will talk about going to England to see the Edinburgh Festival, or going to England to visit their relatives in Cardiff. Yet those same people are affronted when it is assumed that New Zealand is part of Australia. When referring to anywhere in England, Scotland, Wales or Northern Ireland, it's safer to say Britain.

How do *errant* and *error* differ?

It's largely a matter of connotation. King Arthur's knights were referred to as errant when in general they seemed to be involved in praiseworthy projects. Whereas error usually means to make a mistake — and it could be serious.

The words err, errant and error all come from the same ancestor, the Latin *errarer*, meaning to wander or stray. And their exact meanings in English do not differ much from one another.

Error and to err mean to depart from what was meant to happen or what would have been sensible, and instead to cause something different to happen. Often this means someone had made a mistake, been incorrect or strayed from accepted standards. This can be seen as a somewhat negative thing.

But virtually the same word, errant, is often perceived as a quite noble thing, though such a view isn't strictly accurate. King Arthur's knights errant were described in that way simply because, in wandering around in search of adventure, they were departing from the normal standards. It was not a form of judgement to call them errant, simply a statement of fact. Their lifestyle departed from their contemporaries' norm.

A Melbourne Cup winner was named *Ethereal*. Where does that name come from?

Ethereal means delicate and almost as light as air. It comes from the Greek *aitherios*, which means to burn. It is related to the ether — the spaces high in the atmosphere where it's as if all content is burnt and empty and there's just floating nothingness.

The same word was used in connection with a chemical compound called ethoxy-ethane, which is an anaesthetic known as ether, presumably because if the anaesthetic is applied to you, it's as if you're floating in the upper reaches of the atmosphere.

Q **What does the word *ethicals* mean when it is a noun?**

Ethics is the branch of knowledge that deals with human duty and moral principles. When abiding by those principles a person is said to be an ethical person. The noun ethicals is a different word. It is a medicine or drug that is not advertised to the general public because it is only available on a doctor's prescription. That situation is becoming confused by the media advertising of certain prescription-only drugs to the public, who are exhorted to ask their doctor for them. Many people think this inappropriate and undermining of a doctor's experience and decisions — it is not ethical to advertise ethicals.

Q **Does anyone understand *eudaemonism*?**

Quite a number of people understand it, since it is the name of a philosophical concept that has quite a substantial following. But the straightforward definition is a bit confusing: the normative centrality of living well. The philosophy was first proposed by Aristotle and given the name eudaemonism, which in Greek means aided by a good genius. Those who promote eudaemonism believe that the chief good which can exist within man is a state of happiness. So we could define it another way by saying: Eudaemonism is a system of ethics which evaluates actions in terms of their capacity to produce happiness. Or: Eudaemonism means flourishing by nurturing the feeling of wellbeing. Note, you must not keep yourself happy by creating circumstances which make someone else unhappy — that is not part of the deal.

Noel Coward's Mrs Wentworth Brewster may well have been a eudaemonist. Each evening 'beaming with goodwill, she'd just slip into something loose — and totter down the hill' to the bar on the Piccolo Marina.

**What is the difference between an *executioner*
and the *executor* of a person's will?**

Nearly all words relating to execute and its derivatives come from
the Latin *sequi*, to follow. *Sequi* is the grandfather of whole pages
of English words like sequel, sequence, persecute, pursue,
consecutive, consequence and execute. All of these have something
to do with following, or following through, or proceeding to
completion.

In that context, execute means to follow a plan and carry out a
project. To administer the project and make sure it is carried out,
there is an executive. To carry a person's life to its conclusion
might involve an executioner. And to carry out the wishes of a
person's will there is likely to be an executor.

 Is there a difference between *expire* and *expiration*?

Some credit card transactions ask for the expiration date,
which to some people sounds as if the credit card is breathing out.
The verb expire means to cease, to end, to come to a finish or to
breathe out. The noun expiration means the state of doing these
things. Asking for the expiration date of a credit card isn't exactly
wrong, it's just being orotund and clumsy. An expiry date would
do, but to some businesses that doesn't sound grand enough.

There seem to be different meanings for the word
faggot. **What are they?**

It's a very strange word. Faggot comes from the Greek *phakelos* meaning a bundle, which is basically what the word originally meant in English — a bundle of sticks gathered out in the wild, or perhaps stored in the household as firewood.

But there was a side issue. Religious heretics, witches and people perceived to have social or sexual aberrations were often burned on a bonfire. The blaze would normally be built from a pile of faggots, so the word faggot developed a connotation of being connected with heresy.

A bundle of twigs isn't an attractive-looking object and it can be a burden to carry, so the term crept into being a term of abuse, especially of a crabby wife. On *Till Death Us Do Part* Alf Garnett used to call his spouse 'you old faggot'.

The word also crops up in at least three other areas. Faggots are a kind of rissole made from minced liver and breadcrumbs and although it's not entirely clear why they're called that, it may be because the various ingredients are usually bundled up inside a wrapping of animal stomach.

Then, dating from about 1916, criminal slang in the United States started to include the term faggot meaning a homosexual man. The word gradually went into more or less general slang use. The explanation for this usage lies with the punishment of those outside the 'norm', which included homosexuals.

A kind of embroidery is called a faggot. Originally faggoting was gathering threads into bunches that resembled little bundles of twigs. The name developed to describe other kinds of stitches.

When the word faggot went into wide use in the United States in the mid-20th century it was often abbreviated to fag, which brought up another complication.

The American abbreviation fag, short for faggot and meaning homosexual, has nothing to do with either of the British words fag, meaning a cigarette, or the junior boy who does errands for a senior boy in a school. Both those British words are derived from flag, meaning tired and drooping. The schoolboy has his normal work plus errands for the senior, so he is overworked and flagged or fagged. And a cigarette hanging from someone's lips can look droopy and tired, so it too became a fag.

Incidentally, the German word for bassoon is *Fagott*. This elegant instrument is usually made from beautiful sycamore wood, but to some unkind person in Germany centuries ago, it looked like a bundle of sticks.

 Is the expression *few and far between* a quote?

Yes, it comes from a poem by the Scottish poet Thomas Campbell, who wrote:
What though my winged hours of bliss have been,
Like angel-visits, few and far between?

He wrote the lines about 1840 and they have cropped up a thousand times since in weather reports about intermittent showers.

 Is a surname which begins with *ff* just an affectation?

Not at all. The system of lower-case letters and upper-case letters to which we have become accustomed wasn't always like that. There was a time when the use of capital letters wasn't consistent, and the way of showing a word's or a name's beginning was simply to write the initial letter twice. Hence a surname like ffoulkes or ffrench. Families with such names are proud of them, since they denote an unusual level of antiquity.

It must be remembered however, that if a name begins with a doubled initial letter, *they must both be lower-case*. To write Ffoulkes or Ffrench is inappropriate and inaccurate. The double ff is there instead of a single upper-case F and must not be muddled up with it.

Q **Where does the word *finicky* come from?**

It's a close relative of the word fine, in its sense of being excellent, well organised. From fine there developed the word finical, which we don't hear now. Finical meant concentrating rather too much on detail, and becoming excessively particular. By the 1800s finical had become the more slangy finicky, meaning fussy, paying attention to trivial detail.

Q **Why is it a *fig* that people don't care about?**

If, in the 16th and 17th centuries, you stuck your thumb between the next two fingers and pointed at someone, this gesture would have been called a *fico* — the Italian word for fig — and indicated contempt. Gradually the meaning of the gesture extended beyond people and towards other things. In Shakespeare's *Merry Wives of Windsor* Pistol says 'a *fico* for the phrase'. Fig gradually replaced its Italian version, but the meaning retained its overtones of being small in value. Anything not worth a fig was of little value, hardly worth even making a contemptuous hand gesture.

Q **Why is someone described as being *as fit as a fiddle*?**

The word fit hasn't always meant active. In the 17th century it meant finely built and suitable for its purpose. This could well be said of a beautifully made violin, and often was — sometimes also fine as a fiddle. By the time of the 19th century the word fit was beginning to gain a sense of also being physically efficient, and came to be applied to the men who wielded the fiddles.

In an earlier era, long before electricity, a solo fiddler was frequently the only provider of music in the street, and at a banquet or a party, fiddlers provided the music — to eat by and, above all, to dance to. To do all this required energy — a fiddler had to be fit. So being as fit (well-made) as a fiddle and being fit as a fiddler started to slide together. People like alliteration, so either phrase is pleasant to say. People like abbreviation too, so the phrase settled into fit as a fiddle. In both its forms the saying has been around a long time. Sherlock Holmes said it. And in the previous century the Fezziwigs' party in Charles Dickens's *A Christmas Carol* has an excellent depiction of a busy solo fiddler who was certainly fit.

 Why is empty talk called *flannel*?

Flannel is a soft, warm fabric but it has gained an extra meaning of useless talk and evasive words. A place in Egypt called Fustat specialised in making a fabric of cotton mixed with some flax. The fabric, known as fustian after its place of origin, was used very widely. But although it looked quite good, its reputation gradually withered because it was showy-looking but without substance. People used the fabric's name, fustian, to describe anything pompous or worthless, anything that looked or sounded more important than it actually was.

Fustian began to fade from use, and flannel came into favour. It's a better fabric than fustian (it's made of wool) and, although bulky, folds easily and can be used for padding. Gradually, flannel replaced fustian and as the fabric changed, so did the words. Instead of using the word fustian to mean pompous and empty, people rather unfairly used the word flannel instead to mean talk with very lightweight meaning, just filling in a space, like folded flannel being used for padding.

Q **Who originated the saying *a fly in the ointment*?**

     The Bible. It is inspired by Ecclesiastes 10:1 — 'Dead flies cause the ointment of the apothecary to send forth a stinking savour.'

Q **Was Alf Garnett responsible for the expression *foreign muck*?**

He may have popularised the phrase, but it was certainly not a new concept — people are often suspicious of unfamiliar foods. Such an attitude can be traced to AD 100 when the ancient Roman writer Juvenal expressed dislike of everyone and everything outside his own immediate circle.

Alf Garnett was a fictional character played by British actor Warren Mitchell. The TV show *Till Death Us Do Part* was first seen in 1965. It eventually became immensely popular for many years and imitation versions were made in Holland and Germany, and eventually the United States in 1971. The American version was called *All in the Family* and the central character was Archie Bunker.

Alf Garnett specialised in shock-value put-down phrases. He referred to dark-skinned people as coons, called his wife a silly old moo and his son-in-law a randy scouse git. Most of these expressions were clever adaptations by the scriptwriter of existing phrases.

In Garnett's view foreign muck included avocados, lemon grass, tandoori chicken, lasagne, sushi and aubergines. People who lived in England as long ago as the 1920s report that although the phrase foreign muck was well within the common vernacular, it was a shock to hear Warren Mitchell announcing it loudly on television, the moment anyone mentioned pasta or pizza.

So we can conclude that the attitude towards foreign muck had existed for over 2000 years but that Alf Garnett certainly made the expression popular.

Q Why are newspapers, magazines etc. sometimes referred to as the *fourth estate*?

Historically in Britain the three main bastions of power were the Crown, the House of Commons and the House of Lords, and they were referred to as the three estates.

The expression fourth estate referring to newspaper reporters was believed to have been coined by Edmund Burke in the late 1700s but there is no evidence in any of his writings that he did actually say it. So the credit for the expression goes to the first person whose published works include it. In 1828 Lord Macaulay wrote, 'The gallery in which the reporters sit has become a fourth estate of the realm.' This appears to mean that what we nowadays call the media was developing a kind of power that was subordinate to, but more noticeable than, the power of the traditional three estates.

Q Where does the word *franchise* come from?

France. Besides every New Zealand adult having the franchise (the right to vote at elections), you hear the word in connection with shops that carry a famous name but are locally owned, and suburban hamburger bars.

The word franchise comes from the same word as the name of the country France. France used to be called Gaul but was taken over by a European race known as Franks, whose name became attached to the new country. Franks meant free men, so France meant a free country. Thus franchise means to be given the freedom to do something (e.g. vote in elections, sell a particular kind of vacuum cleaner, etc.).

G

 British television programmes sometimes mention a *gaff* and a *drum*. What are they?

The etymologist Eric Partridge believed the slang term drum was originally the Romany word for someone's dwelling, house or address. It moved into English with that meaning, and then developed a secondary meaning of having a tip-off or special knowledge. If a criminal has had a good look around a property he intends to rob, or if he has stashed a girlfriend inside there to work as a maid, then he has drummed the place.

Gaff, a very old English word meaning a carnival, is used in Cockney slang about someone's house, usually when that house is being drummed, presumably because when the robbery takes place there will be action and activity. (Gaff is not to be confused with gaffer, meaning grandfather or boss.)

So drum, meaning dwelling and/or having inside information, and gaff meaning carnival or busy house, can be used in conjunction — drumming the gaff. The intent of that expression is more familiar to us in its American equivalent, casing the joint.

 Does a geyser have anything to do with a *geezer*?

It doesn't appear to, although nobody knows exactly where geezer comes from. In Britain, a geyser is pronounced the same as geezer, which adds to the mystery.

One school of thought says there is an old dialect word, *guiser*, meaning an actor, a strolling player, which is connected with guise, meaning appearance or clothes, and the actor assumed dis-guises. Somehow *guiser* came to be applied to an old man or old woman.

A probably better theory is when the Duke of Wellington's troops were fighting in France in about 1811 they came into contact with Basques, who use the word *giza* to mean an ordinary man, a bloke. The military men used the word and it gradually came to mean the same thing in English. And then, for some unknown reason, it tended to drift towards denoting an ordinary man who was getting on in years. Geezer has been in use in English since the mid-19th century, so the dates match up.

 Is there a simple reason why *get knotted* is an expression of annoyance?

The expression is intended to thwart someone, to dismiss them. The admonition get knotted seems to have originated in the armed services early in the 20th century.

Get knotted is actually a variation on get knackered, knackers being a slang word meaning testicles. Therefore getting knackered has a connotation of being castrated, which is definitely a condition of being thwarted and dismissed.

Getting knackered was considered such a severe fate that the word took on a connotation of being ruined or even killed. The word is still used to describe the place where horses are sent to be killed, a knackers yard. The association with decrepit horses is two-fold, since being knackered or castrated was equivalent to being killed, but knacker was also an ancient term for a saddle.

Although the above version is the accepted history of get knotted, there are one or two less scholarly interpretations of an anatomical nature which may be best left uncanvassed.

 What is the connection between a musician's *gig* and a real horse-drawn *gig*?

None. Musicians' slang, and particularly jazz terms, isn't at all easy to research. The slightly casual atmosphere of musicians getting together isn't conducive to nailing down when and where somebody started using certain words.

Gig has been in use since at least 1905, meaning a music performance job. It was commonly used to mean just one night, but has gradually extended so that it can now mean a booking lasting several weeks.

There are two theories about its origin. Ever since the 1700s, the word gig or jig has been used to signify a party or a spree. And because jazz by its very nature often arose from people making music together, sometimes quite festively, the party connotation of gig spread over into a new connotation of job — when musicians weren't playing together just for fun, but were actually being paid.

Then there is the second theory: that classical musicians often refer to a job as an engagement, which could be a violin concerto, a chamber music recital or a full symphony concert. Jazz and pop musicians found this term rather grand, and began to make fun of it by using it themselves, especially when referring to jobs in murky night clubs and venues of a dubious nature. Eventually shortened to gig, it meant exactly the same as engagement — a paid musical performance.

 When someone *gives up the ghost*, what ghost are they giving up?

Many cultures subscribe to the concept that there are two parts to a human being: the physical body, and also the life force that inhabits the body and makes it into a person. The expression give up the ghost derives from the Jewish idea of people having an immaterial ingredient as well as their physical body. You'll find it in Chapter 11 of the Book of Job, which is where a translation problem starts. The King James translation uses the word ghost to mean the non-material part of a person's life force, and also to mean the active essence of God.

This has become something of a worry because over the centuries the word ghost has taken on another quite different connotation. In later centuries it came to be used in English for two things: (1) the spiritual immaterial part of a living person, and (2) the soul of a dead person which manifested itself to the living world, and was nebulous because it had no physical body.

So there can be confusion with the phrase give up the ghost which, in Job. 11:20, appears as: 'But the eyes of the wicked shall fail, and they shall not escape, and their hope shall be as the giving up of the ghost'. Here it means 'to die' in the sense of surrendering the spirit without which the physical body cannot continue living.

Although the two connotations of ghost have some similarity, they are also confusing. Because of this deviation, some more modern translations of the Bible use the word spirit both in the Book of Job and in the Book of John, where ghost also occurs. Some branches of the Christian church deliberately use the word spirit and avoid ghost.

Q **Whatever is a *goliard*?**

Not a word you hear every day but it does exist. It was heard much more commonly in the 13th and 14th centuries and described educated jesters who could make up satirical verses in Latin, on the spot. They were roving scholars renowned for their riotous behaviour. Is such a man available today? Maybe if the Latin requirement were omitted, Jim Hopkins could get a job as a *goliard*.

Q **Is *google* a real word?**

Not really, though it is one of the most recognised signpost words in the world. The Google search-engine on the Internet was invented by Larry Page and Sergey Brin in 1998. The name was chosen because it evoked the similar word googol, which is a real word — a mathematical term denoting a figure followed by 100 zeros. This 100-zero association evoked an image of the Google search-engine sweeping through hundreds of thousands of search options. (It is also believed that Page and Brine had in mind to tease the CEO of competitor Yahoo, whose name was Koogle.)

The Google search-engine has no known connection with the other word googly, which is also a real word. It's a cricketing term describing an off break bowled with a leg break action.

 What purpose does *good* serve in 'He's coming home for *good*'?

Like many words in English good has more than one meaning. Obviously its usual meanings are commendable, desirable, praiseworthy. Back in the 1500s the original full saying was for good and all and in that context good and all were both functioning as reinforcers and intensifiers — meaning for ever, completely and finally. It is now rare to hear the full phrase for good and all but for good fulfils the same purpose — to intensify.

 Does New Zealand really have something called a *gooey-duck*?

Indeed yes. The gooey-duck is a member of the clam family, a bi-valve mollusc with an unusually long and large burrowing foot. It can burrow nearly a metre into the sand and a big specimen can weigh up to 5 kilograms. This odd creature is found in some coastal waters of New Zealand, mainly around the South Island.

Its real name is *Panopea generosa* and its common name is geoduck (derived from dig deep in the dialect of native Americans on the American coast where the big clam is also found.) That name has been corrupted by metathesis — the middle of the word reversed — and comes out as gooey-duck.

 How did Americans come to invent the word *gotten*?

They didn't. Its origins are in British English as the past participle of to get. The word must have travelled to America in the 1600s and remains in use there but curiously has virtually disappeared in its place of origin, Britain. As a past participle gotten is now regarded as a totally American expression, though remnants of it are found in English words such as forgotten, begotten and ill-gotten, all of which are related to the old 15th-century *gotten*.

When British actress Vivien Leigh was playing a classic English woman in *The Elephant Walk*, she became ill and was replaced by British-born Elizabeth Taylor. But by then Taylor had lived in the United States for many years and sharp-eared critics were nettled that in one scene she inadvertently said gotten, which a classic English woman would never have done.

 If *graffiti* is plural, why isn't a drawing on a wall called *graffito*?

It's not uncommon for a word from one language to be corrupted when it crosses a border into another language. For instance, media is also plural, but is often used to refer to just one thing — say television — which correctly should be medium. During the Word Cup controversy of 2002 some people rather resented their first hearing of the word stadia and felt there would have been nothing wrong with stadiums. Strictly speaking, a single drawing on a wall could be called a graffito and several offerings would be needed to constitute graffiti. But English-speaking people seem more comfortable saying graffiti for every wall decoration, however many of them there are. The *Collins English Dictionary* now acknowledges that *graffiti* can now be regarded as singular — when speaking in English.

 What is the sense in taking something with a *grain of salt*?

The saying has survived intact from ancient Latin *cum grano salis* — with a grain of salt. Quite simply it meant that some foods were more palatable after the addition of a little salt — another version of the notion that a spoonful of sugar helps the medicine go down. The phrase, which has been used in English since the 1600s, has come to mean that there may be just a small piece of truth in what you're being told, but you have some reservations, and if you had some salt nearby that might make the proposition easier to swallow and believe.

 Whatever happened to the word *gramophone*?

It simply went out of fashion. The appliances and devices that now reproduce sounds from CDs and cassette tapes are in fact gramophones, but are called something else. It all began in 1873 when sound was captured on wax and could be played back on a machine which turned the little grooves back into music or voice. Initially this was known as a phonograph or victrola, then gramophone, from the Greek for sound captured and written onto a recording.

Throughout many improvements in the 20th century — the invention of the flat disc, the addition of electricity, extending the playing time, adding stereophonic sound, digital recording and devising compact discs — the essential purpose of the original invention remained exactly the same: reproducing captured sound from a portable source. But new names took over, such as record player, stereo, even music centre.

(see also **Walkman**)

Q **Does being on the *gravy train* have anything to do with gravy?**

It does mean a train, but not one which carries actual gravy. Gravy is one of the many slang terms that come in and out of fashion meaning money — spondulicks, bikkies, the tin, the readies, folding stuff, etc. In American slang during the 1920s the word gravy had a run of popularity meaning money, based on the idea that meat was daily sustenance, and gravy was a pleasing addition.

When railway workers looked at their work roster and

discovered that they were scheduled for a short-haul trip that was not a huge effort but paid the same as the difficult long-haul duties, they described that day's service as being on the gravy train — a day's work that wasn't too long or too hard. Gradually the expression became more generally applied and now means a sinecure, a situation where personal rewards come easily in return for very little effort.

 Q **Does the song *Green Grow the Rushes-O* have religious significance?**

Some people ardently believe it does, but there is little concrete evidence about exactly what significance — and many different 'interpretations'. That most recognisable version ('one is one and ever more shall be so') wasn't published until 1893 when it was called an 'English country song' and little is known about it.

The song is certainly full of biblical and astronomical imagery but time and usage have made some of the lines unintelligible. Diligent speculators can announce that the nine bright shiners means planets but some really convoluted reasoning is required for the April rainers and the six proud walkers and quite a lot of the rest.

There is a plagiarised pagan version you sometimes hear about the triple goddess, the silvery wheel, and the nine-foot circle, but that doesn't help much.

We need to be careful when saying what these old songs 'mean' because the words get corrupted over several centuries' use (e.g. 'The Twelve Days of Christmas', see **calling birds**). This appears to be the case with 'Green Grow the Rushes-O'. The 12 apostles and the 10 commandments and the four gospel makers could be seen as obvious, but the lily-white boys and the symbols at your door are not. Whichever interpretation people were told first, is the one they believe.

Just for the record, here is one interpretation which combines those symbols that appear to be widely accepted with some of the beliefs held about the remainder. The result is a weird mixture of

Jewish imagery, Christian imagery and astronomical features. There is no scholastic authority to back up any of these:

12 for the 12 apostles;

11 for the eleven who went to heaven (minus Judas);

10 for the ten commandments;

9 for the nine bright shiners (could possibly be a set of bell rings);

8 for the April rainers (this *might* be a reference to the constellation of Hyades which was eight stars and was sometimes known as the rainy Hyades because of rains coming in April. Or it could be Gabriel and the Archangels);

7 for the seven stars in the sky (*perhaps* Ursa Major);

6 for the six proud walkers (could be a corruption of waters, thus referring to the pots used by Jesus at Cana, turning water into wine);

5 for the symbols at your door (could refer to the books of Moses, or may be a reference to the Jewish *mezzuza* which all Jewish houses have on their doorpost to show that this is a house watched over by God, though it normally contains more than five prayer verses);

4 for the gospel makers (Matthew, Mark, Luke, John);

3 for the rivals (possibly the Father, the Son and the Holy Ghost, though the word rivals doesn't fit at all and may be a corruption of another word);

2 for the lily-white boys (may represent Jesus and John the Baptist, though it's rather odd they should be clothed all in green. Or it may be a reference to the constellation of Gemini, the twins, green being a reference to the coming of spring);

1 is one and all alone (the Jewish Jehovah, the Almighty God).

The *Journal of American Folklore* believes that the entire song arises from the Hebrew chant of the 12 numbers, a form of which is found in the Passover service that Jews have observed annually for several thousand years. That Hebrew chant, which is called 'Who knows one', has references to the five books of the Torah, the seven days of the week, the patriarchs, the matriarchs, the tablets of the Law and other strictly Jewish imagery. The much later development of Christianity appears to have resulted in a mixing of some Christian imagery with the ancient Jewish imagery.

Besides the original Hebrew chant, there was a German version of the 'Rushes' song in the 1500s and a Latin version in the 1600s. The English-language version seems to have picked up bits from all the previous versions.

But people can sing the song, enjoy it, put scholarship aside and stay with the 'interpretation' they're happy with. Nobody else's is any more certain than your own.

Q **On a film crew, why is one person called a *grip*?**

The term originates in the United States where the film industry as we know it began, using a lot of people with backgrounds in theatre. The scene-shifters in theatre were called grips because they physically gripped the scenery and moved it around, creating the environment in which the drama was to take place.

On film sets, there was seldom the same necessity to shift scenery around to a timetable, but the same term, *grip*, came to refer to someone who did a similar job: he or she was in charge of adjustments to the set, placement of props, building platforms for important features or perhaps for the camera itself. If the camera is to move, the grip will lay the tracks the camera will roll on, and get them absolutely exact. If a scene needs to be shot from slightly higher than the existing tripod, the grip is responsible for locating another bigger tripod.

The grip has become more or less one of the cameraman's extended hands, which is quite a responsibility. In spite of the odd-sounding name, the grip is a quite crucial person in the making of a film. The cameraman doesn't usually leave the camera but when he looks through the viewfinder and the scene doesn't look exactly as he wants, he will ask the grip to fix it up. If the film involves large numbers of people and sets, there will be a key grip who supervises the other grips.

Why are people involved in something experimental called *guinea pigs*?

For many years guinea pigs were used in laboratory experiments because they're small, easy to handle, easy to feed and they breed quickly.

Since the 1920s their name gradually became associated with anything or anyone who was the subject of an experiment. But the most famous use of the expression came during the Second World War when pioneering New Zealand plastic surgeon Sir Archibald MacIndoe did miraculous restorative work on badly burnt fighter pilots in particular. Many of his patients belonged to an organisation set up for their welfare after their operations: it was called the Guinea Pig Club because some of MacIndoe's work was seen as breaking new ground. From then on the term became widely used to describe anyone who was in a new situation, even if it wasn't exactly experimental.

 Okay then, how did *guinea pigs* get their name?

They are rodents, properly called *Cavia porcellus*. The *porcellus* bit suggests that they do have pig-like qualities: they're short-legged and stout and make little grunting noises. Their common name is a complete mistake — guinea fowl do come from Guinea, on the coast of Africa, but guinea pigs don't. The family of animals called *Cavi* actually originates in South America, and the little animals were introduced into Europe soon after Europeans learned that America existed. The most generally accepted explanation for the guinea part of their name is that, during the 1600s, British sailors brought them into Britain and sold them for a guinea (£1 plus 1 shilling).

Q What is a *gurn*?

It means a grotesque face, deliberately pulled to look bizarre and awful. The word has been in use since the 14th century in northern England and Scottish dialect, and is thought to be a variation on grin.

Q Where do we get the word *guru*?

From the ancient Indian language Sanskrit. The word is used in the Hindu religion to signify an elder or teacher, and is used in English to mean anyone looked up to as a source of wisdom.

H

 When describing someone's place of origin, why do we say he or she *hails from*?

There was an ancient nautical practice of attracting or hailing a passing ship to ascertain its port of origin or of departure. From that came the expression I hail from or he hails from.

Q **Why are aircraft kept in a *hangar*?**

Curiously, the word has been in use much longer than aircraft have. Early zeppelins were sometimes kept hanging in a large building but the word hangar pre-dates that. By the mid-19th century hangar in English meant a large building with open spaces inside it which was used for housing carriages. Hangar is a corrupted version of the French word *hangarage*, meaning a very big garage. When it moved into English, the last three letters were lost, and the initial silent French h was pronounced, so the word became hangar and that's how it has stayed. William Thackeray used the word in his novel *Esmond*, published in 1852. After doing duty describing housing for carriages, the word became a convenient name for the large buildings where aircraft are put to rest.

Q **What is the origin of the term *hanky-panky*?**

The origin lies in Latin, but there are several degrees of separation. If the Roman Catholic mass is said in Latin, the consecration section contains the words *Hoc est Corpus* ('This the

88

body'). When old-time magicians wanted to pronounce a so-called magic spell before they carried off a conjuring trick, they often recited a 'spell' in fake Latin, which was actually a phony version of this segment of a Latin prayer from the Mass: *Hocus Pocus, Toutous talentus, vade celenta jules*. From that we get hocus pocus, which came to mean trickery and something that seems like magic but is actually false.

The term hocus pocus remains in English and its meaning hasn't changed. But it has also developed into two other words. One is hoax, which means a joke based on something false. The other is the term hanky-panky. So the original Latin gave rise to a joke version which engendered another joke version. Hanky-panky includes the hocus pocus meaning of trickery of some kind, but has developed its own reference — to surreptitious sexual activity.

 Why do we say people who are faintly cross have the pip?

This is really weird. There is a poultry disease which causes the birds to pine and wilt away. Its name comes from the Latin *pituita* which means phlegm and in English it's known simply as the pip. In past decades, when more people kept poultry, the pip was a fairly recognisable word. If a person was out of sorts or in some way abnormal, they too were said to have the pip. Gradually the expression's meaning drifted to mean sulky or bad-tempered, but the origin is a droopy sick hen.

(The expression might cause confusion in the United States where the pip tends to mean the best, and the seeds inside a fruit are called the pits.)

Q **How do we come to say a situation has gone *haywire*?**

It's an American expression meaning that things have got out of control. The image began when cut hay was first bunched up into oblong bundles called bales, held together with very strong wire looped around them and then tied tight. This wire came in coils which sometimes sprang apart so that the wire went twisting and turning all over the place and was very difficult to control. In addition to this, farmers were known occasionally to use the left-over pieces of wire to do rudimentary mending jobs on broken machinery, etc. Hence there arose the term haywire to mean anything that was either out of control and in a mess, or slightly shambolic, makeshift and poorly organised.

 Some people refer to the lavatories as the *heads*. Why?

Sailing ships had their own version of sanitary facilities. From early times the short horizontal beams on either side of a ship's bow (for hauling up or lowering the anchor) had borne a carving of a cat, and were called catheads. Since they were suspended directly over water, the catheads provided support for direct discharge plus a convenient natural wave-flushing system. So arose the expression going to the heads.

Officers sometimes had use of a chamber pot or oak bucket but the crew were expected to attend to their needs on the leeward side (pronounced *loo*'ard and believed by some to be the origin of going to the loo).

The heads were in the front region of the ship rather than its rear because the ideal motive force for a sailing ship was a following wind. This meant that waste discharged at the bow was blown away from the ship. Hanging over the stern to 'discharge' would have affected everybody in the main body of the ship, downwind.

Long after sailing ships were a thing of the past, seamen continue to refer to a boat's toilet as the heads and the expression is sometimes heard beyond the sea. But the original is plural — referring to the head apparently identifies the speaker as a landlubber.

Q **Is there any reason why people exclaim**
Heavens to Murgatroyd?

The name Murgatroyd has a wonderfully Gothic sound. Sir William Gilbert deliberately used it that way in the 1887 Gilbert and Sullivan operetta *Ruddigore*, where the ghost of Sir Rupert Murgatroyd is prominent.

Decades later, in 1961, an American cartoon television series featured Snagglepuss the Cat. Whether Snagglepuss had ever seen *Ruddigore* we don't know, but whenever he got in a fix, which was often, he yelled out, 'Heavens to Murgatroyd — exit stage left.' This rapidly became a children's catch-cry across the United States and is still occasionally heard now as an exclamation of great surprise.

Q **What is the history of *hell for leather*?**

It means at top speed and especially reckless. The term's origin is surprisingly literal. In the days of horse transport, insisting on high speeds was hard on both the beast and the equipment — the saddles, bridles, etc. In other words, continued high speeds were hell for the leather.

The expression has been in use since at least 1889, when Rudyard Kipling used it in *The Story of the Gadsbys*, where a character says, 'Take the note and ride hell for leather'.

There is also the slight possibility that hell for leather is an ages-old corruption of all-a-lather, describing an overexerted horse.

Q **Being *hemmed in* seems obvious — but is it?**

Not entirely, because hem didn't always mean the sewn edge of fabric.

It comes from an old Belgian word *hemme* meaning an enclosed piece of land. When that word came into English it was slightly modified into hem and retained a similar meaning — an enclosure with an edge or border. Gradually this meaning shifted to refer to just the edge, rather than what it was enclosing. And since edges of garments are seldom left raw, but turned up and stitched into place, the word hem began to be applied to this border.

But when a person is said to be hemmed in there is a leap backwards in language history because they're really using the old meaning of land being enclosed. It fits quite well with the modern meaning in that a garment usually has a hem right around its perimeter, but that hem carries no connotation of restricting the garment. Beyond the *hemme* you would have been on someone else's property and out of bounds.

 Is the process known as *hermetically sealed* connected to the ancient mystics called Hermetics who studied alchemy?

There were once monks called Hermetics, and although they didn't invent the scientific process, there is a connection. The monks were philosophers and followers of the occult scientific writings attributed to an ancient mystic called Hermes Trismegistus. For many centuries people had known about sealing foods without air and the process was eventually named after the Greek god of science, Hermes. There was a connotation of secrecy about Greek gods and also about the philosophic mystics who used the Hermes name. Both the monks and the air-tight seal were totally protected and free from outside influences, linked only because they each had a name derived from Hermes.

Q   Where does the word *hermit* come from?

The English word hermit arises originally from the Greek word *eremia* meaning a desert. That became *eremos*, meaning lonely, then *eremites* — living in a desert. From there it was only a short step to the English hermit — a person living alone and without contact.

What is a *high cockalorum*?

The term arose in the 18th century, based on the high-strutting self-importance of a poultry cock, a rooster. Its base word cock, as in rooster, had the Latin intensifier *orum* added — meaning the rooster of all roosters. Sometimes it was written as high cockalorence. It has come to mean a bossy superior person whose importance may be only in their own estimation.

Some scholars also point to an old game actually called Cockalorum, which was a bit like leap-frog, where the person who could jump the highest was cockalorum, the rooster of roosters.

 Why is a theft sometimes called a *hijack*?

The expression describes a theft of goods when in transit, and its exact origin is buried within the American underworld. One widely accepted theory is that a gunman's usual command to his intended victim was, 'Stick 'em up high, Jack', which became contracted to hijack. In recent years the meaning has also extended. From meaning to steal out of a vehicle travelling somewhere, it can now mean stealing the vehicle itself, or stealing control of it (as in aeroplanes). It is also now possible to hijack something ephemeral: the market, or publicity, or someone else's idea. Or you can hijack a person — someone who is valuable to one organisation can be hijacked away by a rival firm.

 A New Zealand restaurant menu featured *hipi iti*. What does it mean?

Cheese made from sheep milk. *Hipi iti* is Maori for little sheep. The cheese has a cylindrical shape and sheep's milk gives it a sweet, caramel taste. Hipi iti cheese is very similar to feta.

How does a prominent person come to be referred to as *his nibs*?

The origin of the expression goes back to the 18th century, when the word knob was used to mean a person's head, and was also used as slang to indicate the man in charge — the head man, the knob.

The k was slowly dropped off, but the slang meaning stayed the same. By the 19th century the term had crept into university colleges but had changed spelling again, and a superior person was colloquially referred to as nabs.

Sometime early in the 20th century, the vowel changed again, and instead of bossy or superior people being nobs or nabs, they became nibs. Hence His Nibs as a sort of joke title like His Worship or His Lordship, but usually for people whose demeanour or position was rather grand without their having a real title at all.

Q **Is there a connection between *hoik* and *oik*?**

There are three h words describing coughs: a hack is a short, dry rasping sound; a hawk is a rather more moist and prolonged affair, often with a resulting delivery; a hoik is similar — an energetic cough always followed by a significant spit. Hoik is thought to be a variation on hawk, both influenced by hike, which means to lift up and carry. So a moist cough was originally called a hawk and that became a hoik somewhere in the 19th century.

There is a connection with an oik, a yahoo. The word hoik became established as an informal term round about the start of the 20th century. Not long after, a custom developed among British schoolboys of pulling a face and spitting when hearing the name of a rival school, or when a person they didn't approve of was mentioned (exactly like Madame Fanny in *'Allo 'Allo* whenever anyone mentioned Germans). By then an unpleasant cough-and-spit was being called a hoik so it gradually developed that the person being spat about, whose name was mentioned, was referred to as an oik.

The word oik came to be a term referring to someone generally regarded as a yokel, an uncouth nuisance whom the speaker held in contempt.

 From where do we get the term *hoi polloi*?

It is Greek for the masses or the many, and is taken to mean the general public. The phrase has been commonly used in English since at least the 1600s. There has been no attempt to anglicise it; the Greek is still used.

But strangely, it has somehow developed a very inaccurate resonance of slight snobbery — that the person saying it is somehow above the masses of which he or she speaks. The expression is used to suggest the rabble, which is rather different from the masses. (The Latin phrase *mobile vulgus* meaning the ordinary people has, in English, been shortened to the mob, which has a rather different connotation again.)

There is sometimes a vague idea nowadays that hoi polloi means the upper or ruling classes, but nothing could be further from the truth. The confusion seems to arise between hoi polloi and hoity toity, although the two have almost entirely opposite meanings. Hoity toity is a 17th-century expression that began as highty-tighty. It originally meant being riotous or giddy before it moved into meaning superior and stuck-up.

By the way, there's no need to say *the* hoi polloi — hoi essentially means the.

Where does the expression *Hold your tongue* come from?

The expression is as least as old as 1540, where it can be found in the Coverdale Bible of that year. You'll find it in Chapter 26 of the Book of Matthew, where it says, 'Jesus held his tongue.'

New Zealanders call the country *Holland* but why do its nationals call it The Netherlands?

They call it The Netherlands because that's its name. The passports of its nationals say the Kingdom of the Netherlands (ruled by sovereign Queen Juliana of The Netherlands). In earlier historical times the nation was called Holland but the name officially changed in 1815. Only two provinces of the current nation actually carry the name Holland (North and South). And although 1815 seems a very long time ago, there are still people who think the whole country is called Holland. At least one major international manufacturer there, based in the province of North Brabant, labels all its goods 'Made in Holland', which is not actually true, but presumably that name is more recognisable throughout the world than North Brabant or even The Netherlands.

Q How did *holly* become part of Christmas?

The use of holly and other green leaves as a decoration and symbol dates back much further than Christian celebrations. In the Northern Hemisphere greenery (from evergreen plants) has been used around December for centuries as a reminder that more green will come when spring arrives.

According to pre-Christian belief, holly sprigs in the house were a protection against asthma, rheumatism, measles, thunder, lightning and fire. In the fourth century, when the date of Christmas was 'officially' established, the Roman Catholic church recommended that holly be retained as a December decoration, since its sharply pointed leaves could symbolise the thorns in Jesus's death crown and the red berries drops of his blood.

The red berries tend to be missing in a New Zealand summer (though the plastic kind often suffices) but people still hang holly, without always knowing why.

Q What is the background to *home and hosed*?

It means secure, certain to succeed, sure to win. It's seldom used in the present tense, but usually in the past or the future. If something particular happens (to my advantage) I'll be home and hosed. Or because something did happen (in which I was successful) I was home and hosed. The connotation of being certain to win is something of a reversal from the expression's original meaning, which was absolutely literal, and occurred only after all effort had been expended. After hard physical labour, being put under a hose is a certain way of being refreshed and cleaned. So once you're safely home, and hosed, you're in the world of the clean and respectable. In its most literal form, the expression appears to have originated in horse racing, where the term has been widely used for many years. After training sessions and after races, horses are literally taken home and hosed.

There are two other theories. (1) Because hosed is sometimes the way beer comes out of the tap and into a glass, when a job is finished and the feeling is good because the beer has already been poured, someone is home and hosed. (2) In sailing terms, an anchor when lifted back home is hosed down. These theories are not as strongly supported as the racehorse image.

Q When did *hot cross buns* get their cross?

Celebration buns with a cross shape on them existed for many centuries before Jesus was born. In ancient civilisations, the ox was an important beast, and in some places in the Northern Hemisphere an ox was sacrificed once a year during the spring equinox (autumn in New Zealand). There were celebrations, and little cakes would be baked with an image of ox horns on them — usually two pairs of ox horns, one upside-down.

Similarly, there were ancient festivals that celebrated such gods and goddesses as Apollo and Diana, and the festival in honour of the moon had little round cakes with a cross dividing the top into four, representing the four phases of the moon.

So from those two sources, the custom of baking celebration buns with a cross on them was very widely established in many countries before Christianity began to assert itself. People who had become Christian tended to regard all practices like these — worshipping the moon and making sacrifices to oxen — as evil, supernatural and unwelcome. But some customs were so deeply ingrained that trying to eradicate them would have caused trouble. Therefore early Christians adopted these even earlier customs and placed a Christian interpretation on them. People were told that the buns with the bullock horns on them or the four phases of the moon, by happy chance, could also represent the cross on which Jesus died. So gradually they became known as hot cross buns.

(see also **rabbits**, Easter **eggs**)

 A politician who is said to be on the *hustings*, is on what?

Some believe that the word hustings is modern and American but it's neither of those things — it's very English and very, very old. The word comes from two old Scandinavian words meaning house and thing, and the original meaning referred to a large assembly gathered around a chief, a lord or a king. One ancient use of the word was the title of the oldest and highest legal court in the City of London, the Husting Court, which survives to this day, presided over by the Lord Mayor.

But the ancient meaning also widened to refer to political gatherings held in the open air. Over the centuries the word has lost one shade of meaning and gained another. The hustings took on the connotation of a platform or series of platforms from which political candidates presented themselves. You'll find the word used in that sense in Dickens's *Pickwick Papers*.

But it lost another connotation. Originally the people assembled around the chief or the king would have been loyal to him; in other words they were all of one mind. In modern times the hustings are not necessarily outdoors any more, and they certainly don't necessarily involve people who are supporting the cause and the central figure. A modern husting can be indoors and it can be noisy and argumentative. In general the modern use of hustings can indicate that the process of campaigning and electioneering has begun, usually involving touring and often standing on platforms, either indoors or out.

Q What is the origin of *iconoclast*?

Leo III became Byzantine Emperor in Constantinople (Istanbul) in 717. A few years into his reign, he reportedly became concerned that people were venerating icons (figures depicting revered personages) rather than worshipping the actual religious figures they represented. To this end, he began removing or replacing icons, beginning by taking the relief image of Jesus from the gates to his palace, and replacing it with a simple cross. Monks who disagreed with this policy described him, in Greek, as an iconoclast — a destroyer of images. This is thought to be the first use of the word in that context. The word has survived in English for centuries, with the slightly adjusted meaning of a person who attacks a cherished belief or institution and tries to display its weaknesses.

Q Why do we say of that *ilk*?

Ilk is the modern spelling of the old English word *ilca* meaning of the same family. It is related to the modern like. But when used as an adjective the old word means each, as in 'ilka lassie has her laddie'.

 A ship historically connected with Wellington was called *Inconstant*. How could a ship be given such a 'negative' name?

We tend to think of ships having very positive names — *Resolution, Endeavour, Relentless, Impregnable*. But that isn't always the case. Ships over the centuries have had some surprising names: *Insolent, Torrid, Hazard, Dwarf, Doris, Truant* — and *Inconstant*.

It's perfectly true that inconstant means unreliable, unstable, fickle and has meant that for several hundred years. The word occurs countless times throughout English literature, referring to love affairs and to the moon.

But at least a dozen ships built in Britain, some merchant vessels and some intended for war, were called *Inconstant*. America also had some ships called *Inconstant*, so it seems to have been a fairly well-established term, even though it's a name that seems to tempt fate.

The only theory that has been advanced is that *Inconstant* might have been referring to the sea itself, acknowledging the unpredictability of winds, storms, and the fact that the sea can be a noble servant but a very cruel master.

Q What is the origin of the expression *Indian summer*?

It means a spell of fine, sunny weather at the very end of autumn, causing you to think summer is making a brief return. This deceptive warm patch has been referred to as an Indian summer since 1770. There is no problem about what it means, but there is a problem about how it originated.

There are two theories. One is somewhat politically incorrect. Early European settlers to America called the natives Indians, which was rather weird because they're nothing to do with India. In addition, some elements of the American countryside, which the natives took for granted, were strange to the incoming Europeans, who therefore developed ways of describing them. For instance, an unfamiliar local vegetable became Indian corn, because it wasn't like their own corn back home. Hence there came the expression Indian summer, because the warm period wasn't really summer, it was a deception — like the corn, it was a false version. Hence the rather put-down term Indian summer.

In recent enlightened times this explanation has been seen as somewhat embarrassing, so an alternative has surfaced. Some scholars say that the phenomenon of late autumn warmth was noticed mainly in the western areas of the United States, where the Indians tended to live, rather than in the mainly European east. Therefore it was an extra bit of summer enjoyed by the Indians.

Q **What does *in flagrante delicto* actually mean?**

It is Latin for with the crime still blazing. So it means caught red-handed, caught in the act.

Q **Where does the expression *in one ear and out the other* come from?**

We can't be sure that Chaucer actually invented the expression but he certainly used it in 1374 in *Troilus and Criseyde*: 'Oon ere it heard, at tothir out it went'.

Q **What do *interns* actually do?**

The word intern has two meanings. The first is to detain or confine against your will, usually for political reasons, as with intern camps. New Zealand has had these in times of war when suspect people, including foreigners, were forcibly confined.

The second meaning is someone being trained. The word is used with different shades of meaning in different places.

In the New Zealand medical system, hospital staffs include people called trainee interns, who are generally sixth-year medical students on the brink of being fully qualified. Before graduation they work in the hospital but only under the supervision of a group of fully qualified mentors. Medical trainee interns are part of the staff and are paid for what they do. There is little or no likelihood that they will walk away from the medical profession at that point because they're only a short step away from achieving a major goal after years of hard work.

But in some other circumstances the word intern can be used to describe young people, usually university graduates, who are taken on by a large organisation in order to familiarise themselves with its structure. Normally they are not paid and the internship is voluntary labour. If an intern shows any genuine promise, the voluntary period may possibly lead to an offer of actual employment. But there is no obligation either way. The intern may decide that this is not the right career and walk away at the end of the agreed period to start a new occupation.

In this second context, the word intern is not commonly used in New Zealand. Very occasionally a young person will do voluntary weekends at something like a radio station, because they're keen and want to learn the ropes. And secondary schools have a system called 'Work Experience' where senior pupils go out for a couple of weeks, seeing first-hand how the real world works. There are volunteer organisations where mature, experienced people administer a charity, or move into responsible areas where there's a need. And a few organisations have a system of probationary staff, where a person is attached to a firm in a temporary capacity until they've been assessed. But in general, unpaid voluntary labour within a fully professional organisation is not widely known in New Zealand.

 When something is near, why is it referred to as *in the offing*?

Normally anything with off in it suggests that something is going away rather than drawing nearer. But this offing is a nautical term and, as usual with a nautical term, it's used in slightly different ways by different people. In general, the offing is that part of the sea which can be seen either from the shore or from where you are anchored.

Originally in the offing meant a long way away — the distant horizon. But over time, for no known reason, the term has come to mean something relatively close which is likely to appear or happen in the near future.

Q Who invented the idea of an *invisible man*?

The idea of invisibility has intrigued people for centuries, way back to the legends of the Arabian Nights and beyond. Hindus and Rosicrucians and various other philosophies have spoken and written about it and magicians have devised ways of making things seem invisible. But in the English-speaking world the first significant presentation of a 'scientific theory' (fictional) and its outcome into human invisibility was H. G. Wells's 1897 novel, *The Invisible Man*, which made the concept and the phrase famous. Since the invention of movies and television the fascination about invisibility has been exploited many, many times, right up to 2003 with Harry Potter's invisibility cloak and James Bond's 'invisible' car.

Q Exactly what is an *iota*?

See **jot**.

Q Where did the term *Iron Curtain* arise?

The first known use of the term was in 1819, in the diary of Lord Munster. It occurs again in H. G. Wells's 1904 novel *The Food of the Gods*, referring to the way a person is held isolated when in police custody. Since then the term cropped up many times, with slightly different applications. In 1914 Queen Elizabeth of the Belgians said 'a bloody iron curtain' had descended between her and the Germans. The term appeared in Ethel Snowden's *Through Bolshevik Russia* in 1920, and Nazi propaganda minister Joseph Goebbels used it several times; one occasion was reported in newspapers in February 1945.

But sometimes someone uses an existing term that somehow catches attention, and is afterwards credited with having invented the line. Sir Winston Churchill used the term Iron Curtain in a famous speech given to an American college in March 1946, referring to the barrier of secrecy created by those Communist countries who had cut themselves off from Europe after the Second World War. Subsequently Churchill was occasionally credited with having originated the term. He didn't, but he did make it famous.

 What is the origin of *It's the pits*?

There is an immediate mental image of a hole dug very deep, a nadir. But in fact the saying has a much more unsavoury history. Language experts Eric Partridge, Robert Hendrickson and Robert Chapman agree that the term originated among those drug addicts whose pocked and pierced bodies leave only one unused site as a last (and most painful) resort for injection — the armpits.

 Where does the term *ivory tower* come from?

The term ivory tower does occur in the Bible. In The Song of Solomon it refers to someone's beautiful neck, and there is an ivory house in the Book of Kings. But the more commonly used reference phrase comes from a poem called 'Thoughts in August,' written in France by Charles Augustin Saint-Beuve in 1837. There is reference to a retreat where a poet could retire from the world into a 'tower of ivory'. Over the next century and a half, the poet's phrase came to refer to people of position who are aloof from common life and are able to observe it without being affected by it.

Q What does *jankers* mean?

Sometimes presented as jenkers or jangles, it is a military slang term meaning punishment for defaulting. It is believed to be an 'echoic' word, somehow representing the sound of either the noisy bugle call that woke those who were being punished and had to get up early, or dating way back to square-rig sailing days when prisoners and those punished were confined in jangling chains.

The term was used by both the navy and the army. It was heard in the army context during the TV comedy series *It Aint Half Hot, Mum*, when the pianist committed some misdemeanour and was put on jankers.

Q How did *January* get its name?

The main job of Janus, an ancient Roman deity, was believed to be opening up the sky to sunlight each day, then closing it at sunset. Gradually he became perceived as the master of entrances and exits and was thus 'the protector of doors'. In 153 BC, the days following cold December were declared sacred to the god Janus because they were the precursor to spring, the opening of a new seasonal door. Hence, eventually, came the name January for the first month of the new year. Because Janus's appearance could only be guessed at, depictions of him tried to incorporate the belief that he saw into both the past and the future. Thus he was shown with a characteristic that is definitely not admired in modern times — he was two-faced.

Q **Is there any significance in *Japanese car names*?**

Honda is named for the company's founder Soichiro Honda. Similarly, the company founders gave their names to Suzuki (founder Suzuki Michio) and Toyota (founder Sakichi Toyoda.) Mazda was founded by Jujiro Matsuda, whose name resembled the Zoroastrian God of Reason, Mazda.

Isuzu is named after the Isuzu River, Mitsubishi is Japanese for three diamond stones, which form part of the family crest of the company's founding family, and Nissan is Japanese for Japanese industry. Daihatsu, Japan's oldest vehicle manufacturer, has the rather prosaic meaning generator manufacturers.

The word Subaru carries double significance in Japanese. In ordinary language it means unite, but is also the Japanese name for the constellation of six stars known elsewhere as Pleiades (and used as the Subaru company's logo since 1955).

Datsun was originally named with the initials of the three men who first invested — Messrs Den, Aoyama and Takeuchi (encouraged by the fact that *dat* in Japanese roughly translates as very fast). By 1918 the company was producing other models, named Dat-son (as in 'son of Dat'). But because of unease about the suffix *son* being too similar to a Japanese term meaning lose money, the spelling was changed to Datsun. (A New Zealand comic gained some mileage from using the phrase, 'It's raining Datsun cogs.')

Q **How did the word *jargon* come about?**

It came about in a somewhat uncomplimentary manner, since its ancestor is a medieval French word referring to the twittering, meaningless chatter of birds. This indicates, no doubt, the man in the street's attitude towards the specialised vocabulary that belongs to a restricted craft or a specialised subject. Such language tends to confuse anyone else with its use of in-words only others in the group understand.

108

 Why is walking across a street diagonally or against the pedestrian lights called *jay-walking*?

In the United States there is a rather silly-looking bird called a jay which wig-wags when it walks and has a cheeky face. It is found mainly in country areas. So when a rural American comes into the city and crosses the street carelessly, doesn't know how to use go and stop signs, or isn't familiar with pedestrian crossings, city people say he's walking like a jay-bird, which means he's walking all over the place. So jay-walking has come to mean crossing through traffic in a disorganised and wandering manner.

 Why are *jerseys and jumpers* so called?

A jersey is a knitted outer garment that does not have a front closure (as a cardigan does). Although the process of knitting was not invented on Jersey the garment is named after the island, which did originate a fine worsted fabric that resembled knitting.

Another common term for a knitted top garment is jumper. The name was initially used by seamen to describe a loose-fitting all-purpose tunic they could put on over other garments. It wasn't necessarily knitted; sometimes it was canvas. The reason why that garment was called a jumper is lost in antiquity but it is believed that it was called that because there were no fastenings, so it could be jumped into quickly. The name jumper gradually narrowed to be applied only to knitted garments that could be put on in a hurry.

Athletes wearing clothes designed to warm up their bodies before taking part in vigorous sport called these garments sweat clothes, giving rise to the term sweater, often applied not only to a jumper but also to any knitted top garment.

And pullover is often heard to describe a knitted top that is not buttoned or zipped, laced or domed. The garment is complete and enclosed, and is pulled over the head.

Do *Jerusalem artichokes* come from Jerusalem?

No. Nor are they artichokes. The underground tuber is native to North America and was taken to Europe by explorers who thought it had a similar flavour to an artichoke. It is actually part of the sunflower family, and its leaves and flowers somewhat resemble those of the sunflower. Hence the Italians called it *girasola* meaning sunflower, and English speakers mangled the name into Jerusalem — plus artichoke, which they still believed it to be.

The vegetable had troubled times during its early days in Europe. An old wives' tale convinced people that eating it could cause leprosy, because of the ugly and gnarled shape of the tubers.

Q **Is there a difference between *job* and *work*?**

An action or project that involves physical or mental effort is a job. The origin of the word is completely unknown but it is believed to have arisen from horse-and-cart days. A cartload of produce or goods, which was as much as one horse and cart could deliver, was called a job. This survives in the modern expression a job lot, which is used, for instance, when selling all the contents of a house as one total sale, a hangover from it all being loaded into one cart. But eventually a job came to mean anything which represented a finite amount of work.

Tasks undertaken with effort and exertion, either mental or physical, are work. The word originates in the Greek *ergon*, meaning a deed, an effort or an action. The word *ergon* has gone through several changes to finish up in English as work but the original Greek still crops up occasionally in words like ergonomic (still to do with effort). It is difficult to pinpoint a difference between the two meanings, but in general job refers to some specific effort — either one defined task or daily regular employment — whereas work tends to mean effort in general, even the effort expended in doing a defined job ('He works hard at his job.')

Q **Sometimes people don't care a *jot*, but what is it?**

This is an unusual case of one word in English being derived from another language, and the original word still existing in English, side by side with the slightly altered one. The Greek word *iota*, meaning a very small amount, has been modified into the English word jot, with the same meaning. But it is not uncommon also to hear the parent word iota used in English, virtually interchangeably with jot. Both are used, and they mean the same thing. (Jot can be seen in the King James version of Matthew 5:18.)

A secondary meaning has developed for jot: something written down quickly and briefly. It's the brevity which is the clue. This jot also indicates that the jotting is a smaller version of something bigger.

(See also **tittle**)

Q **Why is MP's travel referred to as a *junket*?**

The dessert called junket (flavoured milk set with rennet)has been known since at least the 1500s (Shakespeare refers to it in *The Taming of the Shrew*) and was customarily served in a basket.

The word junket comes from the old French *jonc*, meaning a reed, so the English name of the dessert actually refers to the basket made of reeds or rushes in which the sweet was presented. Because of the dessert's association with feasts (and revelry), the word junket gradually gathered associations of merrymaking. By 1820 junket was being used quite separately from the dessert to describe a pleasure trip, and by the 1880s it gathered a pejorative sense of travel undertaken by officials, at public expense and serving little useful purpose.

Although the term has some history of being used to describe genuinely hedonistic travel for pleasure, it is frequently used unkindly to refer to any kind of travel by a public official, even attending a serious overseas conference.

K

Q   What is the background to the initials *KFC*?

It is an abbreviation for Kentucky Fried Chicken. In 1929 Harland Sanders began the Servistation Cafe in Kentucky, which served nicely cooked poultry. Over the next 15 years plans for a franchise grew, and in 1945 a chain of Kentucky Fried Chicken fast-food outlets was founded in Illinois.

The chain can really be said to have stretched worldwide, because it eventually reached New Zealand in July 1971 — Royal Oak in Auckland. Americans, New Zealanders, and just about everybody else quickly shortened the full name to just 'Kentucky Fried' and the food was especially popular with Pacific Islanders, who sometimes took big loads of it on plane trips back to islands where it hadn't yet been established.

But a growing consciousness of fitness, aided by the Heart Foundation's constant advice about not eating too much fat, gradually made the word fried somewhat suspect. It had to go. So in 1992 Kentucky Fried Chicken changed all its signs, advertising, paper bags and store decoration all round the world and, as discreetly as possible, became just KFC. The recipes haven't changed at all and it's still cooked in fat, but the word fried has been removed from aural identity so customers can put on weight without feeling guilty about it.

Q   What is *ketchup*?

It started out as a sauce made from fish and spices — *ke-tsip* in the Amoy dialect of China. Dutch traders took it from the Orient to other parts of the world, where both the sauce and the name underwent various changes. English people left out the fish, retained the spices and recreated the sauce entirely, using mushrooms, walnuts, cucumbers or oysters. The word first appeared in English in 1690, as catchup. But the biggest boost came when Americans also left out the fish and added tomatoes. So was born tomato ketchup, the only version now widely known (also called catsup or kitchup). Claims from cynics that the commercial ketchup available in New Zealand supermarkets is just the same as the old standby tomato sauce are hotly denied by manufacturers. Tomato ketchup, they proclaim, is much thicker and spicier than ordinary tomato sauce.

Q **Where does the word *khaki* come from?**

Iran originally. It derives from the Persian word *kak* meaning dust or earth, which travelled into the Urdu language in India as *kaki*, meaning dust-coloured. The British military saw the advantages of wearing khaki-coloured garments in battle (instead of red or maroon) and the word has been used in English since 1830.

Q **How should you say *kilometre*?**

Kilo means 1000 and metre is a specified distance, so the law of logic suggests that kilometre (1000 metres) would be pronounced *kill*ometre, with the same rhythm as *kill*ogram or *kill*owatt or *kill*oherz. But there appears to be some confusion between metre and another Greek word ometer, which is an instrument to measure something — as in thermometer, barometer, speedometer, odometer — and those words usually emphasise the central o. Hence kilometre often finds itself mistakenly pronounced as if it were kil*om*eter.

Q How did the word *kindergarten* arise?

The word is in general English use meaning organisations that look after and teach children before they reach the age of going to a 'real' school. But the situation didn't start out that way. Kindergarten was a term associated with the German educator Friedrich Froebel (Fröbel), who in the 19th century devised a 'children's garden' (*Kindergarten* in German) wherein a particular education process was practised, geared to the very young. Their faculties of reasoning and intelligence were developed by various objects, toys, games and exercises.

This was very specific, but the word itself gradually moved into being used about *any* general organisation that cared for very young children. Often these had very similar activities as those promoted by Froebel but not exactly the same. The word kindergarten became familiar in the English language during the 19th century, and it somehow survived the anti-German feeling of the First and Second World Wars.

Q What actually happened to *King Canute*?

Canute (Knut Sveinsson) was a real person from Denmark, who became King of England in 1016 and later was King of Denmark and Norway as well. Legend tells us he was surrounded by sycophants who constantly affirmed that he was the most powerful person in the world — so great, he could command the tides of the sea to go back. Canute was a clever politician who knew his limitations, even if his courtiers did not, so he decided to demonstrate that they were over-estimating him.

He had his throne carried to the seashore and sat on it as the tide came in. He commanded the waves to advance no further. When the waves didn't stop, but started to lap against his feet and his throne, he is reputed to have said words to this effect: 'Let all men know that even if the deeds of kings may appear great there is none worthy of the word power but God, whom heaven, earth and sea obey.'

For some strange reason people who've misunderstood the story want to say that Canute really believed he could command the waves to stay back. Not right. He believed he could *not* command the waves — and thought it was time other people realised this too.

Q How do you *knock someone into a cocked hat*?

It means to win by a very wide margin. A hat with its brim turned up is cocked, as in a gun-lever that is cocked upwards ready for trigger release. The brim can be pinned together to make points: a bicorn is two points, a tricorn is three.

The expression knocked into a cocked hat originates with the game of ninepins, where all the pins were set up with three of them in the shape of a triangle. When all the pins had been knocked down except those three, they were said roughly to resemble a cocked tricorn hat. Thus the ninepins were said to have been knocked into (the shape of) a cocked hat.

Q Does the term *knuckle under* come from fighting?

No. In earlier times the word knuckle was used to mean any joint, including the knee. Bending one's knee and going down to the ground on it in suppliance or capitulation was to knuckle under.

 Why is acknowledging someone else's superiority called *kowtowing*?

In historic China, the all-powerful mandarins demanded that people of lower rank performed *k'o-t'ou* — to kneel and knock the head right down to the ground. Travellers took reports to other parts of the world, and although the actual practice never really took off elsewhere, the word, as kowtow, moved into English, indicating obsequious behaviour.

Q Does *latter* mean the last of two things mentioned, or the last of any number of things mentioned?

The formal definition of latter is the second item out of two items mentioned. Or it is possible to refer to a complete section of something that occurs well away from the beginning, such as the latter part of the film.

If more than two individual items are mentioned, or a whole string of possibilities is offered, and you want to designate the one at the end, the correct expression is the last named. So: 'Out of cornflakes or meusli for breakfast, he preferred the latter.' But: 'Offered tea, coffee, cocoa, milk or orange juice, he chose the last named.'

Q When did things start going down like a *lead balloon*?

It describes something that was a disaster — a joke that didn't get a laugh, a play to which no audiences came, a proposed plan of action with which nobody else agreed. It's sometimes expressed as went over like a lead balloon.

The imagery of the expression is obvious. A balloon, to be successful, has to be as light as possible. Anything made of lead is going to sink. The phrase originated in the United States sometime in the 1940s but swept into popularity very quickly. Some quite graphic variations and other versions have developed from it.

Q *Less* or *fewer*, which word should I use?

Dialectical speech is not noted for strictly following the rules. One rule that is often ignored is the old rule about less being a description of quantity (less sugar) and fewer being a description of numbers (fewer people). In New Zealand (and elsewhere) less is customarily used for both quantity and number, and fewer is hardly ever used at all.

A particular supermarket chain provides the exception. Most big stores have a sign on their express checkout authoritatively announcing '12 items or less', which is grammatically ridiculous. Only one chain abides by its grammar and correctly announces '12 items or fewer'.

Q How did the expression *lettings one's hair down* begin?

It means to relax your standards, and to behave in a way that is somewhat uncharacteristic. The explanation for this expression is really rather boring because it means exactly what it says. And there doesn't seem to be a definite starting point. For a very long time in history, it was a mark of a woman's grooming, breeding and social status always to have her hair dressed up around her head. It was also a hint at her wealth, because elaborate hairstyles usually need to be done by another person. Hair was only ever allowed to flow loose in circumstances of the greatest privacy or intimacy.

That image of hair being up indicating formality and control lasted a long time. An elderly New Zealand woman recalls writing a letter to her mother in the early 1930s telling that she had spent the afternoon playing tennis with friends, but that Mother would be pleased that her hair never came down once.

So initially, when someone said they were letting their hair down, they were doing just that and probably also entering a situation of considerable relaxation. Eventually we came to say it just when someone acted in a lively or unexpected way, whether their hair was actually up or down.

How recent is the expression to *lick someone's boots*?

The concept dates back at least to the 1600s, and it can be found in Shakespeare's *Tempest* with slightly different wording. Caliban says, 'How does thy honour? Let me lick thy shoe . . .'

 Is there really a person called *L. J. Hooker*?

There was. The little girl on the television commercial is 30 years out of date, because Mr Hooker became Sir Leslie in 1973 and died in 1976. Leslie Joseph Hooker opened a small real estate business in Melbourne in 1928. He developed the company's characteristic red and yellow signage, survived the Great Depression and eventually his firm was floated on the Sydney Stock Exchange in 1947. Retaining real estate agencies, Hooker moved into hotel and leisure industries, pastoral holdings and land subdivision and became very big business — the Hooker Corporation Ltd. After Sir Leslie's death, the real estate business was bought by Suncorp Metway, and in 1996 the Hooker organisation acquired Challenge Realty in New Zealand and rebranded it as L. J. Hooker.

Q **In 2001, Buckingham Palace announced the appointment of a new Royal *limner* — to do what?**

The word limner comes from the Latin *illuminare*, to add brightness or light. It crops up in English words like luminous and illuminate.

A limner is a person who illuminates manuscripts, putting glorious coloured initial letters and decorations around the words and adding bits of gold, etc. Royalty, universities and city councils make use of these people to decorate special awards or diplomas. A calligraphist writes in the person's name beautifully, and the document will carry a great deal more visual authority if a limner brings light and colour to its appearance.

Where did the expression *living from hand to mouth* arise?

The imagery is fairly straightforward if you watch babies in action. But when referring specifically to poverty or tight budgeting, the expression was first found in a treatise by Bishop Reynolds of Norwich in 1640. From then on it was in general use, especially during periods of economic difficulty, such as the Great Depression of the early 1930s.

 What is a *little tacker?*

The expression is widely used in Australia and it simply means a young creature, usually a young person as in a girl or boy, though it can also apply to an animal such as a puppy. Little tacker occupies much the same position as little nipper, or little blighter — when said affectionately. It's believed to have originated in a dialect word from Cornwall and Devon but it's not at all clear how it developed in Australia, where it's quite common.

What is the difference between a *lodestone* and a *touchstone?*

They are both actual stones. A touchstone is a flint-like stone, either basalt or jasper, which is used to test the purity of gold or silver. The touchstone is rubbed against the so-called gold and then immediately rubbed against another metal whose contents are known and proven. Both rubbings leave a coloured streak on each metal, and by comparing the two streaks, an expert can interpret the purity or impurity of the gold against which the touchstone was rubbed.

But the word has gathered a meaning of being a criterion and a paragon. To say something is a touchstone means you're naming a standard against which other standards are to be judged.

A lodestone (sometimes spelt loadstone) is also a real stone, an oxide of iron known as magnetite. It is the only substance in nature that has magnetic qualities. This has been known for centuries, and lodestones were in use for ships' compasses hundreds of years ago. The word lode has an old meaning — to guide or a course to follow. It is also found in the word lodestar, which is a star used as a source of reference for navigation. The word lodestone has also gathered a meaning outside its strict definition, in that a person or thing can be called a lodestar or a lodestone by becoming a natural focus of attention.

Sometimes people confuse lodestone and touchstone. It is possible for a person who is a celebrity or leader to be both things. The person could be a natural focus of attention (a lodestone) and also a fine example of how we would like people to be (a touchstone).

But the two things don't automatically go together. One could say of a pop star that the way she dresses and behaves is a lodestone — she attracts attention and even admiration, especially from young people. But many parents wouldn't say she's a touchstone, because they don't regard the standard she sets as very high. They don't mind their children focusing attention on her, but they don't want them actually to copy her and her standards!

 Why is an American *loft* on the ground floor. Shouldn't it be up higher?

Anywhere else, it would be. The word loft is derived from the German *Luft* meaning air, and is applied to places that are high: the gallery where a choir or organ can be placed in a church; the storage room for hay, above a stable; the raised structure that houses pigeons; the space directly underneath a roof where a loft apartment is situated. For unknown reasons, American usage has moved the word loft downwards, to describe apartments even at street level, and although a building would normally have only one loft, American apartment complexes might present a whole row of lofts.

From where do the terms *lord* and *lady* come?

As a term of secular rank (meaning not the biblical sense, where Lord can mean something rather different) these two words have been around for centuries. Lord can mean a man of high hereditary rank or a man with bestowed power (such as Lord Bishop, Lord Mayor). The word comes from the ancient English word *hlaford*, meaning keeper of the bread. His wife would be called Lady (in the British system men always share their title with their wives but women never share their title with their husbands) which comes from the old English *hlaefdige*, meaning the kneader of the bread. (The *dige* bit at the end of that word still survives as dough.)

How did the saying *lost his marbles* originate?

In the decades at the end of the 19th century and the beginning of the 20th, playing with marbles was a powerful fashion among children. Quite complex terminology described many different games and kinds of marbles, which could become treasured possessions. The loss of a special marble — either in competition or by any other means — could cause major distress to a young owner. A well-known story in the early 20th century told of a boy whose marbles were stolen by a monkey, and the phrase that someone's marbles had gone with the monkey became an indication that they were in distress. The equating of going crazy with losing a precious marble had appeared in print by 1902. The concept took hold in Canada, where by the 1920s losing one's marbles had become indicative of being not quite sane. During the 1930s, when the expression drifted to the United States, it was also used by English novelist P. G. Wodehouse. It was also heard in the positive — to have all one's marbles, meaning to be smart and savvy. By 1950 both terms had become fairly universal.

When a person is angry, how have they *lost their rag*?

Many kinds of shirt are supposed to be tucked in. If the ones that are meant to be tucked in leave their moorings, some people see this as evidence of loss of self-control. Get my rag out is a variation of get my shirt out — become angry and lose control. Lost my rag is another version of the same idea. There are also lose my cool (meaning composure), lose the plot (forget the sequence of events), lose my marbles (become irrational and forgetful), lose my cookies (lose physical control, and vomit), and, the ultimate, lose it (lose control of everything).

 How did the word *lotto* come about?

Obviously it is connected with lottery but it has a slightly different origin. The word lottery is believed to come from Dutch, referring to people holding numbered cards from which random winners are drawn. With a meaning something like this, lottery has been used in English since the 16th century.

The shorter word lotto is a close relative but it appears not to be just an abbreviation of lottery. It is an Italian word — or at least an Italian version of the lottery word. The Italian language likes words that are short and sharp with a double consonant in the middle and a vowel at the end.

So the French have been saying their version, *loto*, and the Italians have been saying *lotto*; the Italian version crept into English use in the 18th century.

 Most people know what a *lurgy* is, but where did the word come from?

A lurgy is an unspecified illness or germ. It has many applications, covers all kinds of distress caused by illness and is sometimes referred to as 'the dreaded lurgy'.

In 1897 a German firm was founded, specialising in metal and chemical processing, and named Metallurgische Gesellschaft. This firm used five letters of its name, lurgi, as its cable address, and when it separated into various companies in 1919, one firm, which concentrated on gaseous products, was actually named Lurgi. It may have made the gas used against the Allies in the First and Second World Wars. The name Lurgi was well known to industrial chemists and because the company was involved in metal manufacture, that word was printed on the containers it made, including those containing poisonous gases. So among the Allied military in both wars, there was a mind-association between the words lurgi and poison gas.

When *The Goon Show* first went to air in Britain and the Commonwealth in 1951, startled radio audiences encountered what grew to be called 'alternative humour'. The Goons, specialising in creative lateral thinking, wrote and broadcast such icons of appealing nonsense as the 'Legend of the Phantom Head Shaver', the 'Affair of the Lone Banana' and the 'Dreaded Batter Pudding Hurler of Bexhill-on-Sea'. In their first broadcast (28 May 1951) when the Goons were still called 'Crazy People', they mentioned issuing lurgi pills.

In November 1954 they broadcast a story called 'The Lurgi Strikes Britain', which was about a mysterious and somewhat ridiculous disease. There is a school of thought that the Goon writers' fevered brains invented the word as a deliberate corruption of allergy. We don't know exactly if the Goons were thinking of German gas cylinders when they broadcast their story, but we do know that several of the Goons had strong military associations, so it seems more than likely.

The word lurgy went into the language almost immediately. Because initially it was only heard spoken on radio, it emerged in print with various spellings. It has been used ever since to mean a slight illness — or worse, a dreaded lurgy.

Q Were there real *McDonalds* who made hamburgers?

Certainly. In 1940 two brothers called McDonald opened a small but efficient fast-food outlet in San Bernadino, California. They had a distinctive red-and-white colour scheme, and their hamburgers and milkshakes were so successful that they had a sign up saying, '1 million sold'. They introduced sauce dispensers and created a system of assembly-line food workers, one to each task, so hamburgers were ready all the time and customers didn't have to wait. The McDonald brothers opened their first branch store or franchise in 1952 and eventually had more than 10 other fast-food outlets bearing their name.

In 1961 the McDonalds were bought out by a businessman called Ray Kroc, who within a year had franchised over 200 more McDonalds 'restaurants' and then went on and on. According to American writer Bill Bryson, Kroc ordained that McDonald's hamburgers were all to be 3.875 inches wide, weigh 1.6 ounces and contain just 19 per cent fat. The buns with seeds must average 178 seeds. (In 2003 the London *Observer* reported that the number of seeds had gone up to 198.)

By 1994 the McDonalds organisation bought more potatoes and beef than any other organisation in the United States and was serving 25 million customers a day in 68 countries, causing it to be decreed the world's largest owner of real estate.

McDonalds arrived in New Zealand in 1976 with a single outlet at Porirua. By 2000 there were 144 outlets throughout New Zealand selling 80 million burgers a year (and 30,000 outlets worldwide).

To make the burgers, each year 4 million kilos of New Zealand beef is transformed into hamburgers, over 7 million kilos of potatoes become McDonalds chips, 36 million lettuces are shredded and New Zealand hens provide 9 million eggs to be cooked.

 How is it that a suit of armour and what comes into the letterbox are both *mail*?

Chain mail and postal mail — the words seem to be identical twins, but they have different fathers. In a suit of armour, the sections that move are generally made of linked mesh or small overlapping plates called mail. That word is derived from the Latin *macula*, meaning a spot, a circle, a mesh. It can be found in the modern word immaculate, meaning tidy and without spots or blemishes.

But the letters in your letter box get their name from Old German, where the word *malha* meant a bag or wallet, and the word was used to describe the bags in which messages and letters were carried from place to place. The name of the bag became transferred to mean the contents of the bag, which in English finished up as mail.

 What is the difference between a *Man of Kent* and a *Kentish Man*?

Kent is believed to be the oldest county name in England, dating back to 55 BC. The county of Kent has a river called the Medway passing through it, and for many centuries that has divided the male population: a male born on the west of the Medway River is called a Kentish man, and the man born on the east side of the river is called a Man of Kent. The distinction is quite firm, and there are cases of fathers and sons, or brothers, having been born in different hospitals so that there is one of each within the same family.

Being born east or west of the river makes no difference to women born in Kent — they are all called Fair Maids of Kent. This term commemorates the daughter of a 14th-century Earl of

Kent, Lady Joan, born in 1328, who eventually married Edward Prince of Wales, the Black Prince, and became Joan Plantagenet, the mother of Richard II. She was very beautiful and was always called The Fair Maid of Kent. Women born in Kent still are, seven centuries later.

 How did the expression *man of straw* arise?

There is no clear answer to this. In centuries past, some men would hang about courtrooms and make themselves available as witnesses who, if paid, would say anything required and swear it was true. To signify this, they had a sort of code that lawyers would recognise: they wore some sprigs of straw in their shoes. This kind of witness was of course a fake, not to be believed, hence the connection with a man of straw, who was not strong, reliable or dependable. There is not a great deal of evidence for this story.

More generally, the term man of straw is taken to be self-explanatory, referring to a person as if they were an actual dummy, someone whose external qualities don't match up with a weak interior, a sham, an argument that can easily be defeated, with no more substance than a straw doll.

 Why do people say someone has *marbles in their mouth*?

Sometimes the people who say this are confusing two different expressions. Marbles in the mouth goes back to the legendary Greek figure Demosthenes in 300 BC, who was reputed to have overcome a speech defect by standing by the sea, putting pebbles into his mouth and forcing himself to speak over the noise of the waves. In time he became a great orator. That appears to be the origin of the idea that putting pebbles or marbles in your mouth and forcing yourself to speak in spite of them improves your pronunciation and articulation.

Many people will remember that Rex Harrison, playing Henry

Higgins, put marbles into Audrey Hepburn's (Eliza Doolittle's) mouth in the movie *My Fair Lady*, though it must be pointed out that George Bernard Shaw did not write that piece in his play *Pygmalion*, on which Lerner and Lowe's 1956 musical was based.

We must remember that Demosthenes and Eliza Doolittle both took the marbles out once they'd mastered the knack of rounding their vowels. They never actually spoke with marbles in their mouth; they practised speaking with them.

Confusion sometimes arises with a quite different expression, plum in the mouth, which generally indicates that a high-class pronunciation is being used.

Nowadays, saying that someone is speaking with marbles in their mouth often seems to mean that someone is speaking indistinctly. So the original intention of the exercise — putting marbles in the mouth in order to improve articulation — has been altered.

There's an old joke about how to be a good public speaker: fill your mouth with marbles and make a speech. Every day, take out one marble and make a speech again. When you have lost all your marbles, then you'll be an effective public speaker.

Q **What is the *Marquess of Normanby* most famous for?**

George Constantine Phipps, always known as Lord Normanby, was an experienced parliamentary and regal administrator. He was appointed Governor of New Zealand in 1874 and held that office through difficult times in the nation's history — the abolition of provinces, struggles about constitutional questions and the defining of the Governor's discretionary powers.

Whatever legacy his governmental work in the early colony left, subsequent generations seldom mentioned him. Most New Zealanders have never heard of him. But one moment in his tenure remains immovable. New Zealand's national anthem 'God Defend New Zealand' is dedicated to Lord Normanby.

Where does the name of the town *Marton* come from?

The town currently known as Marton was given that name in 1869. When Europeans first settled there in 1859 they referred to the district by its original Maori name, Tutaenui. Unfortunately the word means large pile of excrement, a fact that had begun to filter through by the time it was decreed that the centenary of Captain Cook's first visit to New Zealand be commemorated. This seemed an appropriate time to find a pleasant new name for the growing town. A public meeting was held, and it was decided that the town be named after Captain Cook's birthplace in Yorkshire. And so it came to pass that Big Turd was renamed Marton.

 What is a *maven*?

The word grew to prominence in the United States in the 20th century, referring to a person whose opinion is noteworthy and whose advice is followed. It is from an old Hebrew word *mebin*, meaning knowledge or wisdom. From Hebrew it migrated into the Yiddish *mevin*, meaning being understanding. After a slight spelling change it is now frequently used in American English where it has come to mean an expert and connoisseur.

What is the background to the prayer '*May the road rise with you*'?

It is a popular blessing made famous by its use in Ireland. There are several verses and occasional variations in the words, but the most famous version usually says: 'May the road rise with you, May the wind always be at your back, May the sun shine warm upon your face, May the rain fall softly on your fields, Until we meet again, May God hold you in the palm of His hand.'

This 'Irish' version is widely known but the concepts behind the blessing are Jewish. Early Christian clerics in Ireland frequently took inspiration from Hebrew sources and with that wonderful Irish gift for language were able to restate and transform those that inspired them into what one could call a fluid Irish style.

Close study of 'May the road rise' indicates that much of its inspiration appears to come from the Book of Isaiah in the Bible. The line about the road rising with you can be seen to connect with Chapter 40, the famous opening of Handel's *Messiah*: 'Every valley shall be exalted, and every mountain and hill shall be made low: and the crooked shall be made straight and the rough places plain.' And Chapter 49 says, 'I will make my mountains a way, and my highways shall be exalted.'

Chapter 49 of Isaiah also says, 'neither shall the heat nor sun smite them, for he that hath mercy on them shall lead them, even by the springs of water shall he guide them.' And in Chapter 55: the words 'For as the rain . . . watereth the earth, and maketh it bring forth and bud . . .' can be seen to mean that the sun will shine warmly and the rain fall in the fields.

Chapter 49 also tells the word of God: 'I have graven thee upon the palms of my hands', in which can be seen the image of God holding you in the palm of his hand.

All this is legend, supposition, interpretation and research, rather than stated absolute fact, but careful examination does seem to support the belief that the Irish prayer comes from Jewish base material, lovingly recrafted into a mellifluous blessing, as only the Irish can do.

One version of the prayer on an Irish cathedral wall demonstrates the Celtic and clerical sense of humour. The final line reads: 'May God hold you in the palm of His hand — and not squeeze too tight.'

 Q Is there a term for a person to describe *the members of the family into which that person's child has married*?

For instance, the mother of a married daughter referring to her daughter's mother-in-law. In the English language, there really isn't such a term. Under the definition of kith and kin, none of the in-laws are actual kin because they do not share your blood. They could be kith because that means people close and knit into the family but not necessarily with the same blood.

But if we temporarily turn our back on English, there is a perfect word in Yiddish. The word *mechutonim* is used to mean the members of the family into which my child has married. A daughter's husband's family, who are the daughter's in-laws but, strictly speaking, not the in-laws of her parents, can be referred to as *mechutonim* and this will indicate that there is a connection to that family by a marriage somewhere. At least everyone who understands Yiddish will know that.

Mechutonim (which is the plural form — in-laws) is a bit tricky to spell in English, which doesn't have the Yiddish 'ch' sound, and Yiddish vowels are somewhat variable (sometimes the word comes out as *machutonim*). The male singular is *mechuton* and the female singular is *mechutenisten*. It is probably easier (when speaking in English) just to put them all in one group and use the plural, *mechutonim*.

Q Did J.R.R. Tolkien invent the name of *Middle-earth*?

No. Tolkien certainly invented the setting and the language and the characters and stories but he didn't invent the name. The term middle earth is a very old expression, dating back to ancient Scandinavian mythology and drifting into Anglo-Saxon English as *middangeard*. It was perceived as a mystic place, somewhere between heaven and hell.

Middle-earth is actually mentioned in *Beowulf*, one of the oldest pieces of English writing, dating from the late 10th century. As a professor of Anglo-Saxon studies Tolkien would have been very familiar with this work. The term can also be found in Shakespeare's *Merry Wives of Windsor* (Act 5, scene V) when someone speaking about Falstaff says, 'I smell a man of middle earth', indicating that it is not a very desirable place.

So Tolkien took a known name, then developed a huge and quite different imagery around it. Such borrowing is a perfectly valid practice. Many famous and classic works of literature have done this — *Gone with the Wind*, *The End of the Golden Weather* . . .

Q **Why is a person who makes hats called a *milliner*?**

The word is derived from *Milaner*, meaning someone from Milan. In earlier centuries the city was famous for its manufacture of fancy goods, which travelling salesmen took all over Europe. Eventually the designation from Milan settled onto just hats, and in time transferred to the people who made them, whether they were from Milan or not.

Q **Where would I find a *misocapnist*?**

You'd find several in the lung cancer department of a hospital and some more in ASH. There are three ingredients in the word: *miso*, *kapos* and *ist*. The Greek for dislike, even hatred, is *miso* or *mis* (found in such English words as *misogynist*). The Greek word for smoke is *kapos*. And *ist* usually means a person with the qualities mentioned earlier in the word. Therefore, a misocapnist is a person who hates smoking and smoke.

Q **Was a *Molotov cocktail* named after him, or did he throw one?**

The Russian statesman Vyacheslav Mikhailovich Skryabin adopted the name Molotov in 1906 in order to escape from the Imperial Police. Molotov is Russian for a kind of hammer. He was the Prime Minister of the Soviet Union from 1930 to 1941, and was Minister of Foreign Affairs during and after the Second World War.

Molotov didn't invent the so-called Molotov cocktail, nor was it a Russian invention. Spanish soldiers were reputed to have used the device in 1936. In 1940 the Russians were fighting the Finns, and it was the Finns who refined and developed this home-made anti-tank bomb: a bottle filled with inflammable fluid and sealed, with a wick poking out the top. The wick was lit, then the bottle thrown at a tank. When it broke the liquid ignited and spread all over the tank plating.

This was widely adapted for use by the British Home Guard, and Mr Skryabin, aka Molotov, was intrigued with the device and organised the manufacture of similar devices in Russia. Thus the 'bomb' became known by the Russian foreign affairs minister's nickname, Molotov.

Q How did the word *mollycoddle* arise?

Generally meaning to indulge, mollycoddle is a combination of two words. Coddle exists as an independent word — to treat gently. Coddled eggs are cooked just below boiling point. A coddled invalid is not allowed to do anything strenuous. Jane Austen writes in *Emma* (1815) about a person being coddled.

The woman's name Molly is usually an informal version of Mary. At times in history it has had unfortunate associations with low life — for some time a molly or a moll meant a prostitute.

But the word Molly also has a soft and cuddly sound, and from the 18th century onwards it was used to identify a person who was overgentle and overprotected — a milksop, a wimp.

Over time, the two words drifted together, with molly becoming an intensifier for the existing term coddle, and by 1849 you'll find Thackeray using the combination word, mollycoddle.

Q What does *momentarily* mean?

It means for a very brief space of time — for a moment. It does not mean soon, which makes a nonsense of the frequently heard announcement, 'The aircraft will take off momentarily', which actually means it will take off, zoom into the sky for just a moment and then come down again.

Why are there several different meanings for the word *mortar*?

The English word mortar arises from the Latin word *mortarium*, meaning a bowl in which things are mixed. Hence from the two Latin words *pinsare*, to crush, and *mortarium*, a bowl, we get pestle and mortar.

Various substances have been mixed in a mortar, including mixtures that are used in putting up buildings, and over time the word was transferred to the contents of the vessel. Therefore mixtures of cement, sand, lime, etc. are referred to as mortar, because they were mixed in a *mortarium*. (This transfer of meaning, where the name of the container is used to describe whatever is in the container, happens quite often in English. See **mail**.)

Then an interesting second transfer took place. Once the mortar has been mixed, a builder will take a lump of it onto a square board with a handle underneath, from which he trowels it into place. Thus we get the name mortar-board for the academic hat with the flat square top which resembles the mortar-layer's tray.

Since the 16th century there has been a weapon known then as a mortar piece which appears to have been called that because it is short and wide-bored, somewhat like a bowl.

Q **Is there a difference between a *motor* and an *engine*?**

There is no clear and definite answer. Every engineer and mechanic who reads this is going to have a different opinion, because usage varies from one circumstance to another. In general (very general), a motor is a machine that converts a form of energy into mechanical energy to produce motion and an engine is a machine that converts a form of energy into mechanical work. But neither of those definitions works properly and many variations and contradictions arise from them.

There is an impression that a motor is connected with movement, although one commonly hears the inside of a car referred to as either an engine or a motor, maybe because it produces a form of work which eventually, but not directly, makes the wheels go round. In other words, it's associated with both work and motion. And a train is customarily driven by an engine, which undergoes work that later results in movement.

But a refrigerator is normally referred to as having a motor, and a refrigerator doesn't move anywhere.

All of them convert one form of energy into another. In general (again — very general) it is possible to say that a motor is involved in actually moving something somewhere, even as a fan or a washing machine does. And an engine causes work to be done which sometimes may eventually result in motion but in its direct form is static.

 Who originated the term *movers and shakers*?

The term dates from *Ode*, the best-known poem by 19th-century English poet Arthur William Edgar O'Shaughnessy. He was referring not to activists but to artists:

We are the music makers,
We are the dreamers of dreams,
Wandering by lone sea-breakers,
And sitting by desolate streams; —
World-losers and world-forsakers,
On whom the pale moon gleams:
We are the movers and shakers
of the world for ever, it seems.

In an era of corporate lions and electronic wizards, the meaning of the term seems to have moved slightly. It is still used to describe those who take the even tenor of our lives and disturb it — people who challenge established laws and morals — but nowadays the movers and shakers tend to be political or corporate people, not artists. Originally, the term meant people like the Beatles and Colin McCahon rather than Winston Peters or Bill Gates.

Q **Why do *movies* have their production date in Roman numerals?**

Movies were being made from the 1890s onwards, but in the early decades of the industry, the movies appeared not to have copyright dates on them.

From 1915 onwards, bigger 'classic' movies were being made. In the 1920s the United States government passed a law decreeing that all movies issued had to have their date of production included in the credits. This didn't please the movie industry, which, for various reasons, didn't always want people to know when a film had been made. Sometimes a movie was held back and released a year or more later, pretending that it was just new. Or a movie released for the second time may not have wanted to parade its actual age. So the movie people obeyed the law and included the date of production, but deliberately put it in Roman numerals to make it difficult to work out.

Comparatively few people can understand Roman numerals, particularly long ones. Only those with a classical inclination can read them at speed. So the movies obeyed the law, but escaped easy date identification.

Q **How did we gain the designation *Ms*?**

The English word mistress used to be said when addressing all women. It evolved into several other forms which designated the marital status of the woman being addressed: Mrs — a married woman, Miss — an unmarried woman and Miz — a rustic American honorific that seems mainly to be Mrs but can sometimes be equivocal: e.g. 'Miz Lillian' (Carter, married, mother of a president) and 'Miz Scarlett' (O'Hara, unmarried).

By the late 1940s some women were beginning to agitate for a prefix that didn't identify their marital status. Ms started to be promoted in the early 1950s as a possible non-discriminatory courtesy prefix for all women. It was believed to be a modern version of the old-fashioned American Miz. This was a minor puzzle of semantics versus usage, since Mrs, Miss, Miz and Ms are all variations on exactly the same word — mistress.

Ms did not have a smooth passage into the language and was not generally accepted until the 1970s. Some women didn't want to be connected with it at all. New Zealand Prime Minister Helen Clark announced that she would be addressed as Miss, rather than as Ms, or Mrs with her husband's surname. The *New York Times* initially refused to publish the word until 1986 when it gave in.

In the meantime, mistress had slipped sideways to mean a woman in a sexual relationship with a man to whom she is not legally married. The situation thus described became commonplace but there was some resistance to the word mistress, which gradually became replaced by partner.

Q **What is the origin of the word *munted*?**

It is used to mean something is wrecked or mutilated, damaged, broken, not in good shape, stupid or gormless. In the early stages of its popularity munted was current only among drug users, to mean absolutely overdosed and completely, hopelessly out of control. From there it seems to have widened to mean just drunk (which is a little less dangerous) and then again to refer to anything that is out of order or abnormal.

The origin of the term is very vague. There is a possibility that it is connected to the derogatory and insulting South African term *munt* or *munta*, meaning a black person. There is also a possibility that munted could have arisen as a version of those weird characters *The Munsters* in a long-ago TV series.

Having grown as an expression within 'yoof' culture, munted is now in general currency, with a fairly innocent meaning of being just out of order.

How did the world come by *Murphy's Law*?

There are several different stages to the story. In ancient Yorkshire a concept with which most people are familiar was crystallised into the phrase sod's law, which described the frequency with which things can go wrong in ordinary life (e.g. when you're in a hurry and you push a door you're supposed to pull). Sods' law is considered to be a corruption of God's law: in God's law everything goes well, but in sod's law everything goes wrong.

In 1949, on an American air force base, Captain Edward Murphy was supervising a technician who was preparing a test of human tolerance to speed and was installing some essential sensors. Captain Murphy discovered that the technician had put each one of them in upside down. At that point, reports vary about what Captain Murphy actually said. It was either: 'If there is any way to do it wrong, he'll find it,' or 'If there are two or more ways to do something and one of those results in catastrophe, then someone will do it that way.'

The air base projects manager came to hear of the incident and when he was describing it to a news conference a short time afterwards, he referred to the captain's remark as 'Murphy's law'. The name rapidly went around all the other aerospace engineering personnel and found its way into *Webster's Dictionary* in 1958.

Captain Murphy's statement actually allowed for some optimism. After the original incident, he realised that the sensors looked the same both ways and therefore could be inserted upside down, so he redesigned them. This eliminated the possibility that they could be put in the wrong way. A possibility for disaster had been averted.

The final stage in the story seems to lie with the science-fiction author Larry Niven, who from 1964 wrote a very popular series of books in which occurred something called Finagle's law, which was a very much simplified version of Captain Murphy's statement. Niven wrote it as: 'If anything can go wrong — it will.' That's the version now almost universally known as Murphy's law, having developed from sod's law through Murphy's law to Finagle's law, but still credited to Murphy.

A maverick, largely unsubstantiated version assigns the origin to a Professor Murphy at Long Island University who asked all his students to throw a pie up to the ceiling and see how many stuck and how many fell face down on the floor.

 Is *Muzak* a real word?

It has become a real word, albeit originally an invented trade mark, like Vaseline, Nugget and Biro. And it's older than we think; playing music into lifts was first patented in America in 1922 by George Squier, who started doing just that.

The only explanation of the word's ancestry is that apparently George Squier was intrigued with the trade name Kodak, which was a completely invented word which means absolutely nothing. So a similar formula was used to come up with a cute word combining part of music with the same ending ak, resulting in Muzak, a trade name which was so commonly used that it is now in dictionaries, while the commodity itself haunts us every day. No restaurant, lift, shopping mall or call-waiting service is complete without it. Offerings of Muzak can be classified as red, green or blue — depending on the time of day or type of purchasing at which it is aimed.

 What does the word *mythering* mean?

It's a dialect word with at least five different spellings: meither, mither, moither, moide and myther. To myther means to bother, to become a nuisance, to perplex, to bewilder, to nag or to pester. People from the Midlands and northern England tend to say it to their children, 'Don't myther me.'

The word is so old that its origin cannot be pinned down. It has been in common use since at least the 1500s and can be found in Christopher Marlowe's play *Tamburlaine the Great*, published in 1590. But where it came from before that nobody knows.

**When a person feels ill, are they *nauseated*
or *nauseous*?**

The condition of nausea is named after the feeling of being seasick
(from the Greek *naus*, meaning ship). Nauseated used to be part
of a verb, requiring an auxiliary in front of it — 'I became
nauseated' or 'I feel nauseated'. But over time, influenced mainly
by American use, it has shortened to a kind of adjectival adverb: 'I
am nauseous', which means the same as 'I am nauseated' but is
marginally easier to say. Thus nauseous has become the norm.

 **Is there any connection between the words
nautical and *naughty*?**

No, there is no connection at all. The Greek *nautikos*, based on
naus, a ship, gives us the English nautical. But naughty is quite
different. It is a genuine English word, made of up two parts: *na
wiht*, meaning no thing. The spelling of that changed slowly to
naught and the meaning varied a little bit to mean of poor quality,
worthless rubbish.

There was a slow development into two slightly different
directions. The spelling and meaning of naught remained exactly
where it was, meaning nothing, a trifle (you hear it on *Coronation
Street* all the time in its Lancashire form, nowt). Naught, of poor
quality, gained an extra meaning of bad behaviour, wickedness.
This was the meaning Shakespeare intended when he wrote, in
The Merchant of Venice, 'So shines a good deed in a naughty world'.
Over time, naughty paled in meaning to refer to misbehaviour.

What does this mean: *Ne'er cast a clout ere May be out?*

It's an old British proverb, usually said as a kind of rule that people (and especially children) should be careful not to abandon winter clothes too soon, until the warmer spring weather is reliably established. Clout is an old word meaning cloth or garment. The word May in the proverb has caused confusion, since some people believe the admonition to mean don't abandon winter clothes until the beginning of June, when May has finished. But according to the BBC Nature Research Unit, the word may refer to the tree, a type of hawthorn. This gives the saying a slightly more flexible application: winter clothes can be shed when the may tree comes into bloom. Nature knows better than any calendar when the warm weather has become stable.

 Is there such a place as a *neck of the woods?*

The word neck can be used to mean a narrow stretch of land. During the 19th century the phrase neck of the woods came into use in the United States to mean a place where there was a gap in a forest and a settlement had grown up. But in time neck of the woods came to mean any settlement or area, whether it was among trees or not.

Is it true that *news* **means** *north, east, west, south?*

Apparently not. There is a popular belief that the word arose from a picture of a weathervane, showing NEWS on its points and that the initials gradually amalgamated. But scholars deny this absolutely, and say that news is simply derived from the old English word *niwes*, meaning that which is new.

Where did the *'nick'* come from in *nickname*?

It comes from the old word *eke*, which in simple terms meant also. The word was used to mean that a person had an additional name, an eke name. So for instance a queen called Elizabeth might also be known as Gloriana or a queen called Mary might be commonly called Bloody Mary. That second name was an addition to their basic name.

Over time, an eke name gradually became a neke name, and then eventually, a nickname. A nickname now means an informal name, commonly used about a person instead of the name they might have on their passport or their bank account.

 Is there a connection between being *nicked* and being *in good nick*?

A large number of words and expressions have developed from the very basic activity of cutting a notch in wood — a V-shaped notch called a nick.

Though superseded now, those V-shaped nicks were crucial in such activities as archery, point-scoring in sports and counting. A nick could be done very accurately or it could be messy. If it was accurate, the action was a good nick. Gradually being in good nick became a complimentary description applied to inanimate things, such as machinery that performed well, and then it spread to include humans or indeed anything at all that was efficient and neatly done.

Cutting a neat, accurate V-shaped notch was admired, so the phrase in the nick meant at exactly the right moment when something crucial or precise happened. Until the end of the 1500s, in the nick was sufficient. Gradually two extra words were added so it became in the nick of time.

The notch in wood, if it were cut quickly and firmly, also carried an image of chips flying away rapidly so eventually we have swift movement or speedy departure becoming nicking off.

Some expressions are connected with thievery and custody:

nicking something; being arrested or being nicked; being placed in custody or in the nick. The origin of those terms is not 100 per cent certain, but they do seem also to be related to the V-shaped notch.

When a notch is made in an innocent piece of wood, it can hardly be to the advantage of the wood. Hence something has been taken away from the wood — it is no longer complete. It has been reduced in value: it has been nicked. Thus is engendered a rather convoluted network of words connected with thieving and being caught. From there it's not a long step to the place of incarceration, the nick. Describing the lock-up itself as the nick appears to have begun with the military round about the turn of the 19th century, when the term was used for the guard room or detention cell. In time it moved to the general justice system and is now widely used to mean the prisons administered by the law of the land.

The V-shaped notch of wood has a lot to answer for. But there are many other nick words which have nothing to do with wood: a kind of marble, being in the nude, a noise made by a horse, the devil. (See also **nickname**.)

Q Was there ever a real *nigger in the woodpile*?

Originating in the United States, this derogatory expression came to mean a concealed but important fact, or a catch in a proposal — a hold-up that prevents something sailing smoothly.

A likely source of the expression says it arose through black slaves escaping from the southern states by hiding on freight trains under piles of wood and supplies on railway wagons that were heading north. So sometimes there really was a black man in the woodpile, which came as something of a surprise at the other end.

142

 Q Why we do we say someone is talking *nineteen to the dozen?*

The expression means to talk very fast or for a long time with no indication of stopping, and has been in use for a long time. Richard Sheridan's *Journals* used exactly these words in 1785. Obviously the imagery is that a person can speak nineteen words in the time anyone else would only manage a dozen, but there's no known reason why it should be 19 rather than 18 or 20. Perhaps it's only that 19 seems to sound right.

Q Why is drinking alcohol sometimes called having a *noggin?*

The word *noggin*, meaning a cup or glass to drink from, has been in use since the 1630s. Gradually the meaning has undergone a transference of meaning, so that sometimes it means the container — but sometimes can also mean that which it contains. 'Going out to have a few noggins' usually means you're going to drink the contents of a few noggins.

Nog*ging* with 'ing' is a building term for horizontal pieces which strengthen a framing.

 Q What does the word *nous* actually mean?

Not to be confused with the French *nous*, this one is pronounced nows. It's a term widely used to describe someone who has acumen, brains or ability. Although regarded as a slang term (similar to having smarts), in fact the word has an impeccable classic pedigree. It's used today in exactly the same ways as it was in ancient Greece, where it comes from. *Nous* was Greek for mind and intellect. Plato used it to mean complex matters such as 'the system of divinity springing from blind nature'. It moved into the English language denoting intelligence and understanding, but with the added connotation of someone's having 'horse sense'.

O

Q **Why is the letter *O* used as a number?**

Speaking this alphabet letter (instead of a number) often occurs in phone numbers such as O800 and O25. And James Bond is called double-O seven — 007. The probable reason is that O and zero do look the same, and that people are generally lazy, so the one-syllable O is easier to say than the two-syllable zero.

In the days before STD (subscriber toll dialling) when all 'distance calls' had to be made through operators, the New Zealand telephone directory recommended saying O rather than nought when you were giving the operator a number. This was supposed to reduce the possibility of mistake because nought can sound like eight.

Caution is necessary now that we're in the computer age, because a computer keyboard has three O-like characters. There is numeric zero, and also an upper-case O and a lower-case o. It is absolutely essential that you hit exactly the right key. In one incident in New Zealand a computer operator was having a code read out aloud to her, and the person said O when they meant zero. The woman typed in an alphabetical capital O, which was not an intended part of the code and it crashed the operation.

So O can be dangerous, and nought can be misheard. Only zero reliably means what it says!

Q **Exactly what are *odds and sods*?**

Items additional to the main supply are odds — things that are slightly in excess of a given number, or a surplus. The mysterious word sods usually means lumps of turf or soil, but it

143

has a side meaning of something useless and possibly unpleasant.

There are several combinations with odds: odds and bobs, odds and ends, odds and sods. All of these mean things that are miscellaneous and not in a proper order. In general the odds and sods version is used when you wish to describe something useless and even faintly undesirable.

Q **When is something** *off the wall*?

When it is new, completely different from the usual and possibly even a little outrageous. The imagery is said to be from a game of squash, where the ball moves so quickly that sometimes it hits the wall and comes off at a completely unexpected angle, catching a player unawares.

Q **Where does the chant** *Oggie Oggie Oggie* **come from?**

Cornwall. There were and are several British naval bases in Cornwall and nearby Devon: navy training schools, dockyards and Royal Marine barracks. It is believed that men of the sea originated this old word oggie as a slang term for what we call a Cornish pastie, which has been made in Cornwall for centuries. Hundreds of men took oggies down the Cornish mines and the Cornish will tell you that their pasties gave British seamen the strength to sink the Spanish Armada in 1588. And even before that one of Henry VIII's wives wrote a letter mentioning Cornish pasties so perhaps they gave King Henry strength too.

The Cornish pastie, or oggie, needed to be nourishing and durable since it was carried down into the mine, and later heated in a tin bucket over a candle. The pasty was and is intended to be eaten held in the hand. Its fold-over shape provides a firm crust as a holding edge, and because the miners' hands might not be too clean, the crust could be thrown away after eating the main portion. Often there was a meat filling at one end, and apple or some similar dessert-filling at the other end.

The three-fold call Oggie Oggie Oggie is believed to have begun either from Cornish housewives calling out that the pasties were ready, or as an enthusiastic chant by naval men invoking the strength they believed pasties gave them. The famous Welsh entertainer Max Boyce was intrigued with the call and started to use it in his concerts all over Britain. He was also a sports enthusiast and he helped the cry spread to sports matches and develop a return call of Oi Oi Oi! Eventually the custom reached Australia and during the Olympic games the Oggie was often dropped out and replaced by Aussie Aussie Aussie. Other countries in the world have substituted their own name at the beginning and Ja Ja Ja or Si Si Si, etc. as the answer.

It all dates back to the humble but nourishing Cornish pasty.

Q Why is something described as *old hat*?

Virtually everything is affected by fashion and everything gets old. Some, of course, set themselves against trends and are determined not to observe it, but find that, almost against their will, fashion will influence the vegetables available at their local shop, the size of their newspapers, what's in headlines, the shape of their new house and the plants on sale at the garden centre.

But fashion can dictate change that is wasteful and ridiculous, especially in clothes. There have been times when the hat, for a male or female, was of extreme importance. Unspoken forces dictated that the shapes, decoration and fabrics be changed from time to time, and abiding by these changes was of great importance to many people. Women in pioneer New Zealand, struggling with a new and difficult life, would still eagerly await ships carrying fashion news from London about what kind of hats should be worn.

The consciousness of fashion in hats still applies. Fashion decrees that baseball caps are worn back to front, and now encourages knitted beanies that mothers begged their children to wear when they were seven. But many hats are made of very durable materials — wool felt, Leghorn straw, or stitched fabric — and it is not at all uncommon for the hat to outlast the fashion.

Well-made headgear is often in good condition when its place in fashion has passed by, so although it is perfectly serviceable, it has become an old hat. In some eras a person seen to be wearing something out of fashion became an object of great scorn. These people had committed the deadly crime of wearing an old hat.

In time, the saying came to mean anything that was overfamiliar and boring because you'd seen it all before.

Q Whatever happened to the word *Oriental*?

It is a word New Zealanders recognise in the breach but hardly ever in the observance. Immigrants from China began to arrive in the colony of New Zealand from 1850 onwards. Over the decades, when referring to these New Zealanders, the word Chinamen was replaced by the slightly gentler Chinese. Eventually, wider immigration brought people not only from China but also from Taiwan, Korea, Cambodia, Vietnam and Japan — all undoubtedly and identifiably Oriental. In most parts of the world the word Oriental is used to refer to all these people.

But for some unexplained reason, New Zealanders resist the word Oriental and it is hardly ever used at all. Asian is the preferred description, although the vast area of Asia also includes Turks, Russians, Indians, Bangladeshis, Tibetans, Pakistanis, Thais, Nepalese, Iranians, Iraqis and Filipinos, none of whom is Oriental.

Q How does the image arise of holding someone *over a barrel*?

In general, scholars agree that it dates back to a method of assisting someone who has nearly drowned. The poor unfortunate was stretched out over a barrel with their head pointing downwards, so that the water would drain out of their lungs.

Naturally the person in this position was very vulnerable and helpless, and completely under the control of those giving the treatment. Therefore, over time, the expression widened its application to refer to anyone in a position where they couldn't do anything.

There is also a slight possibility that when people in the old days were being flogged they were tied over a barrel to keep them still, but the drowning one is the origin most believed.

 Where are people when they're *over the hill*?

This expression is thought to have begun among soldiers. When someone deserted from the army and walked away from their responsibilities, the other soldiers said he had gone over the hill. But then ordinary people began to use it and the word hill began to mean the effective part of your life, starting when you're a child and going upwards until you become an adult and then travelling even higher as you become good at what you do. But everyone eventually becomes old, so when you start to move a bit more slowly, and you can't work as well, then it's as if you've reached the top of the hill and are now going downwards — over the other side.

 What exactly does *oxymoron* mean?

The word is used to describe a juxtaposition of two ideas that don't comfortably sit together: a weak tyrant or a poor millionaire.

It is a very strange word because oxy means sharp, keen and acute and moron means stupid. Thus, the word itself appears to be an example of internal contradiction — stupidity that is at the same time sharp and keen. This certainly can apply to some oxymorons where a vivid image is evoked by deliberate contradiction, e.g. a living death.

Strictly speaking an oxymoron and a contradiction in terms could, by splitting hairs, be described as slightly different technically. But there's no doubt that the two terms are now interchangeable.

P

 How did we come to describe a situation as a *pain in the neck*?

We came to it through politeness, because pain in the neck is a polite substitute for pain in the bum. The expression indicates that the pain being referred to is mental rather than physical, and it's within yourself — you're the one who doesn't like whatever it is.

The polite version has been in fairly common use since 1910. There are various versions of the original: pain in the bum, pain in the butt, pain in the arse. And some acceptable versions: pain in the elbow, and the New Zealand variation pain in the puku. Adding the word royal makes it even more impressively painful.

Q **Why are people who carry a coffin called *pall-bearers*?**

The word pall is a shortened form of *pallium*, which is Latin for cloak. At some periods of history a person's cloak was draped over their coffin, and this developed into there sometimes being a flag or, when appropriate, a royal standard.

In other cases, the covering can be of a completely different kind. The coffin of film star Rudolph Valentino was covered in a blanket made of gardenias, and the coffin of New Zealand historian Shirley Maddock was covered with a profusion of orchid blooms.

The term pall-bearer is an example of a figure of speech called metonymy, where you name something associated with a concept and, by doing so, intend to include the whole concept. For example, in this phrase 'a law laid down by the crown', the word crown is a shorthand association with legislation and the government system. To say bearing the pall — the cloak — indicates that you are also carrying the coffin under the pall.

Often, there is no actual cloak or cloth over the coffin, but the term pall-bearer remains in use. There may be a euphemistic reason for this: pall-bearer sounds less harsh and a shade more gentle than coffin carrier.

 Sir Walter Scott mentions *pallions*, which means what?

Scott used the word in 'Border Minstrelsy': 'They lighted high on Otterburn, and threw their pallions down'. Robert Burns also used it. Pallion is a variation on *pallium*, which means a big cloak. It comes from the Latin *palla* meaning mantle and is still used in some medical/anatomical contexts where something is described as shaped like a mantle hanging over something else. Pallium is also used in some Christian churches to describe the flowing cloak worn over the shoulders of high-ranking clergy.

So that's what Sir Walter Scott's men were throwing down.
(see also **pall-bearers**)

Q **When did the word *pantyhose* come into use?**

Obviously it's a combination of two existing words, panty and hose. Those garments and those two words had existed for many decades before someone had the bright idea of joining them together.

The word panty is a version of pants, which comes from the Italian word *Pantalone*, which was the name of the eccentric figure in theatrical performances who wore funny elaborate clothes and trousers.

Hose is an old-fashioned word. It comes from the word *hosa*, which originally meant male leg covering of a fairly loose kind, often criss-crossed with ropes or leather to keep out draughts and protect from thorns and twigs.

What we call stockings actually have a different history: they originated in ancient Rome. Made out of beautifully soft goat hair, they originally reached only to the shin like a sort of long sock but over the decades they grew longer and longer. They were only for men, of course; women were expected to be covered up with skirts.

When William the Conqueror arrived in England in 1066 his troops introduced the tube-like leg-covering garments to English men. They were fitting a bit better by then, and the men called them skin-tights. William's son Prince Rufus was known to wear skin-tights that came right to the waist and had knickers built in. These were called stocking pants, so the garment we call pantihose has actually been in existence since the year 1100.

Tight stockings for men became commonplace, and wearing them in outrageous colours and designs became one way for youthful rebels to upset the rest of society. Chaucer comments on this.

We also know from Chaucer that by then women did wear stockings — the Wife of Bath wore red ones. Scholars agree that women had been wearing them for quite a while but nobody knew — unless they saw them in the boudoir. Elizabeth I received her first silk stockings in 1561 and would wear nothing but silk from then on.

Machines to knit stockings were invented during Elizabeth's reign: the leg-cover industry started in 1589 is still going strong today. In general stockings were called hosiery, and for many decades the industry made leg-covering tubes that were separate — one tube for each leg — and generally in only two lengths: mid-thigh for women's daily wear, called stockings or hosiery, and long, long ones for ballet dancers, who had access to specially manufactured tights that joined at the top and kept on going right up to the waist. The dancers reverted to William the Conqueror's word and called them tights.

Around the sixth decade of the 20th century, women's skirts became shorter and shorter, and there was a need for long stockings that came right up to the crotch. So, probably without even realising it, manufacturers came up with a new version of what Prince William Rufus wore in the year 1100.

Then the word pantyhose arrived in 1963 in the US, meaning long stockings attached to lightweight underpants. Sometimes they are still referred to as tights, but pantyhose (or pantihose) rapidly became a commonly understood term.

 ## When people accidentally swear, why do they say *Pardon my French?*

The expression is usually shorthand for 'I've just said something indelicate but I hope you'll overlook it.' The term was first observed in use in Britain in 1916. It seems to be connected with the British troops who fought in France during the First World War. The theory is that because many British soldiers couldn't speak French, they joked that when French people spoke to them vehemently, they could well be uttering swearwords for all anyone knew. Somehow that became twisted into French words equating with swearwords. Hence when one of those was said in the wrong context, the phrase Pardon my French followed it.

In the United States the term was modified to Excuse my French.

 ## Is there any term that describes the four *parents of two unmarried partners?*

No there isn't, if the lovers aren't married. Nearly all relationship terminology is based on the premise of there having been a legal marriage — bride, groom, mother-in-law, divorce, adoption, engagement, spousal maintenance, etc. Take away the marriage certificate and all those terms cease to exist. And even if the young couple was married, there is no easy way of the parents-in-law describing each other (see **mechutonim**).

There are jokey ways out of it, like saying my mistress's mother, or my mother-out-of-law, or my shack-up's mother. But the direct answer is that there is no formal term by which the parents of unmarried people living together can refer to each other.

Q **What exactly is *Parkinson's Law*?**

Cyril Northcote Parkinson was a British writer with more than 60 books to his credit. He had worked in the British Civil Service in the 1920s and 1930s and wrote works on politics and economics as well as a large amount of very successful fiction, including stories that continued the adventures of C. S. Forrester's fictional character Horatio Hornblower.

In 1957 Parkinson wrote a book called *Parkinson's Law*, the main premise of which was his observation that 'Work expands to fill the time allocated for its completion.' In other words, if you allocate half an hour to clean the oven, you'll get it done in half an hour. If you allocate four hours to do the same thing, it will take four hours. Parkinson also created the similar observation that 'Expenditure rises to meet income.'

Q **Is the word *pâté* from the same family as *pesto*?**

No. The old Greek word for sprinkled barley has several modern relations, including pastry, pasta, pâté, pasty (white-faced), paste, pastel (pale) and pastiche (bits and pieces mixed up).

The delicacy we know as pesto originated in Genoa so has an Italian name. In antique times, before there were food processors, pesto was made of nuts and basil leaves and oil, vigorously pounded together into a paste, inside a bowl called a mortar, with a bashing implement called a pestle. The Italian word *pestare* means to pound, as in hit heavily, and the mixture being bashed in the bowl was described by the verb's past participle, *pestato*, meaning that which has been thumped and pounded. Because pounding with the thumping implement was vital, the mixture took on the name of the process that made it, and it became known as pesto.

From the same ancestry comes the word piston in an engine, and also tisane, a herbal infusion where the original vegetable matter has been pounded.

What is the background to *paying through the nose*?

It means paying out too much money for something and the background is very unpleasant. There is only one theory about where the expression comes from: in ninth-century Ireland a general tax known as a poll tax was imposed on every person within the population, regardless of income. If you failed to pay the tax, you were punished by having your nose slit. Thus the belief arose that if you didn't pay the tax, when you were found out, you'd be punished (a) by having to pay it anyway and (b) by having your nose mutilated. So the cost was very high, and you were paying with, by or through your nose.

 Where does the 'pen' come from in *penultimate*?

English has borrowed bits and pieces from many other languages, and the proportion of Latin terminology in English is large. Penultimate uses two Latin words: *ultimate*, meaning final, and *paene* meaning almost. Thus penultimate means almost the end and is generally used to indicate that which comes second to last.

 How do we get the word *pernickety*?

It's a very old Scottish dialect word, so old its exact source can't be traced. But in an odd kind of way it simply *sounds* right — fastidious, punctilious, particular about details and trifles. Americans use a slightly different version, adding an 's' and saying persnickety.

 Who invented *The Peter Principle*?

This first appeared in 1969 in a book entitled *The Peter Principle*, written by Canadian educationists Dr Laurence Peter and Raymond Hull. A study of business, the book contained a line that has often been misquoted since. The original line said: 'Work is accomplished by those employees who have not yet reached their level of incompetence.' This is sometimes repeated slightly wrongly as: 'All members of a hierarchy rise to their own level of incompetence.'

Q   **Whenever and wherever was there *pie in the sky*?**

The phrase is American and dates back to 1911. It is associated with a somewhat anarchistic Labour organisation called Industrial Workers of the World, which started a few years earlier than that, and which was known jocularly as The Wobblies (because of its initials). The organisation paid a lot of attention to migrant and casual workers, and one of its unifying forces was song. Everyone who joined the IWW was given a little red songbook which contained rousing parodies of popular songs, such as 'Hallelujah, I'm a Bum' and 'Nearer My Job To Thee'.

In 1911 they put out a song parody that was directly aimed at the Salvation Army hymn 'In the Sweet Bye and Bye'. The IWW workers took offence at the Salvation Army's implication that there would be joy in the afterlife so long as one remained meek and compliant in this life.

So out came the parody which, instead of the sweet bye and bye, said, 'Work and pray, live on hay, you'll get pie in the sky when you die.' Although somewhat unfair to the Salvation Army, the phrase went into the language very quickly. In time it almost completely lost its sense of religious parody, and instead became a depiction of a dream scenario or an unrealistic hope.

Q   **What is a *pilgarlic*?**

A very old term of contempt, pilgarlic refers to a clove of garlic with its skin peeled off, and therefore to a bald man. Admittedly, a man's bald head does look something like a skinned clove of garlic, but there was also a vague unspoken belief that a man who had gone bald may have suffered from the pox. So saying he had a head like a peeled garlic clove was an expression of pity — and some contempt. A pilgarlic is someone you despise but also feel faintly sorry for.

 Is there any connection between *Ping-pong*, radar and computers?

To begin with, Ping-pong is not a Chinese term. The game is believed to have begun with 19th-century British army officers using the lids of cigar boxes to bat little balls across a row of books on a table. Later, more efficient little bats were made of vellum and the balls were cut from cork. By 1891 the game had been made into a marketed item in Britain, and sets were sold under the names Gossima, Whiff Whaff and Flim Flam. Then an Englishman called James Gibb refined the equipment and in 1900 the brand name Ping-Pong was invented and registered as a British patent. This new name for the game was described as being two 'echoic' words: ping for when the bat hits the ball, and pong for when the ball hits the table. In 1901 the term also became a registered patent in the United States. The game and the name took off.

For a couple of decades Ping-pong was very big indeed worldwide and it still commands a large following, though now it is generally called table tennis. In 1971 an American table tennis team went to China and that gave rise to the term 'ping-pong diplomacy'. It also became clear that many Chinese and Japanese people were particularly good at table tennis so a vague legend arose that the game and the name originated in China. In Puccini's opera *Turandot*, first staged in 1926, the three senior courtiers at the Emperor of China's court are called Ping, Pang and Pong. The names just sound Oriental!

All of the above happened before 1930 so the words were fairly well established before radar began using the term ping for a radar signal, and before computers started using the word ping to indicate that a message needs a reply, and then pong when the return message has been activated.

Q Why is small change called *pin money*?

The term arose in the 14th century when pins were very expensive, and women were given a special allowance to buy them. Sometimes a special bequest was left in wills, just to provide a beneficiary with money specifically to buy pins. Therefore the term pin money was a self-explanatory factual statement, and this usage lasted until at least the 17th century. In a Thomas Vanburgh play of 1696 a character is described as having £200 a year solely to buy pins.

But technology and manufacture gradually advanced, so pins became cheaper, and women with pin money had enough left over, after buying pins, to spend on other things. So the term came to mean small amounts, nothing financially consequential.

Q Is it accurate to say *pissed as a newt*?

No. Few people who say this expression have a clear idea of what a newt actually is. It is a lizard-like creature that resembles a New Zealand gecko. Some species are aquatic and some are not. The reasons for describing anyone as pissed as a newt are mysterious, though it is conjectured that because some newts live in water, this gave someone the fanciful notion of their being totally immersed in 'drink'.

Another theory suggests that because a newt's skin fits neatly over a rather complex body shape, it could have engendered the expression tight as a newt. This later evolved in two separate ways — tight moved away as a stand-alone word meaning drunk, and the word pissed moved in and replaced tight. Any way you look at it, it's an odd expression — real newts never get drunk.

Q **Why is someone described as *po-faced*?**

There are two elements here. The origin of the expression seems to be poker-faced, meaning to assume an expression that gives nothing away — either as stiff and unyielding as a poker standing by the fire, or as unmoving and undemonstrative as a person playing poker and not wanting to reveal what they have in their hand.

But although po-faced is descended from poker-faced it doesn't mean quite the same thing. It can mean either expressionless, or showing stern disapproval and distaste — possibly influenced by the word po being a once common term for a chamber pot.

Q **How did the flower *poinsettia* get its name?**

The flowers are named after the first American ambassador to Mexico, Joel Poinsett. Besides his diplomatic duties, Poinsett was an ardent amateur botanist who looked for unusual plants in Mexico. In 1825 he noticed something growing wild in a Mexican ditch, took it back to his glasshouse in South Carolina, and fostered the plant. Now, in the United States at least 60 million poinsettias are sold each year during December alone.

Q **Where does the name of the game *poker* come from?**

It has nothing to do with the rod you push into a fire, which is named from a German word *poken*, meaning to thrust. The name of the card game is also from German but from a different word altogether, *Poch-spiel*, which means a game involving bragging or boasting.

Q **How did the card game *pontoon* get its name?**

Some words with pont in them are somehow connected with bridges — such as pontiff for the Pope (who is perceived by some Christians as the bridge between themselves and God) and pontoon, a floating vessel that is used for support or for acting as a temporary bridge.

The card game has nothing to do with this. The game aims to acquire cards with a face value of 21 and was properly called *vingt-et-un*. This French term became abbreviated by English speakers into just *vingt-un*, which eventually was corrupted into pontoon.

Q **What is the origin of a ship having a *poop deck*?**

The name comes from the Latin word *puppis*, meaning the stern or aftermost part. In modern times the actual aftermost part of a ship is generally called the stern but the word poop survives as the aftermost and highest deck, often forming a roof of the cabin directly underneath it.

There's no connection with a couple of other poo words in English. The childish words poop and the reduced version poo, for excrement, come from an old Dutch expression meaning a sudden blast through a pipe. And the American expression pooped, meaning tired and worn out, is thought to be simply a made-up nonsense word.

Q **In the expression *power and pelf* what does pelf mean?**

The word dates back to the Latin *pilare*, which means to despoil, and then through Old French as *pelfre*, meaning booty. During the 14th century, the French *pelfre* came into English as pelf, which was a contemptuous term meaning money acquired by somewhat dubious means.

Q **The term *presidential-style campaign* means what?**

Within the various systems categorised under the heading Western democracy, there are two main divisions, parliamentary and presidential. In the parliamentary system, the nation's power is in collective representation. Voters are asked to vote for a party, whose policies are outlined by its various candidates, then the party elected represents the faith of a majority of voters in what that party represents. Those people elected then choose a cabinet and proceed to govern the country by collective cabinet responses, not just the dictates of one person.

The presidential system places considerably more emphasis on the elected president, who although he may be actually appointed by an electoral college after the votes are counted, still more or less single-handedly represents the image of his party.

In terms of campaigning before an election, the parliamentary system, in theory, puts forth candidates who present the policies of their party, and seek votes for that party, more or less regardless of who is representing the various segments of it. A presidential campaign concentrates its energies on the person who seeks to be a political leader.

Each system has its critics. Political scientists will tell you that the parliamentary campaign can result, and has resulted, in a national leader who is actually unpopular, though the party is not. A presidential campaign, heavily built around image, can be criticised as resembling a beauty contest or a talent quest.

One has to point out that the term presidential-style campaign is often allocated by the media rather than necessarily being the conscious decision of the people involved.

 What is the difference between *prevaricate* and *procrastinate*?

Prevaricate comes from the Latin *praevaricari*, meaning to walk crookedly. English has developed the word prevaricate, which means to speak falsely with the deliberate intention of deceiving: to tell a lie.

Procrastinate also come from Latin: *pro*, meaning in favour of, and *cras*, referring to tomorrow. In English it means to defer, to put off.

Why is old music sometimes called a *prick song*?

For the last two or three centuries, a musical score has customarily had vertical lines drawn through the stave, making what we call bars, with so many beats to a bar. But it was not always like that. Ancient music was not written with bar lines. Anyone who has sung Christian plainsong or Gregorian chant or synagogue canting will know how difficult that is to the modern eye — the music just goes on and on.

During the 15th and 16th centuries someone invented vertical lines to divide the tune into measures. In those days a mark was often made by pricking and the word prick had a subsidiary meaning of mark, so gradually sheets of music and songs developed which were pricked or marked with these new-fangled vertical dividers which we now call bar lines.

During that transition time the term prick song was frequently used to mean written music which had been divided into rhythmical bars, as opposed to a written out melody whose regular rhythm (if it had one) was not plainly visible in the writing. The term is no longer used because now most music has bars.

 Apparently there are some fanciful names for a collection of *prostitutes*. What are they?

A group of cats can be called a clowder of cats and many skylarks together are called an exultation of larks. Legend hath it that a group of university men once coined a series of terms that could describe a gathering of ladies of the night. They were: an essay of trollops, an anthology of pros, a jam of tarts, a fanfare of strumpets, a peal of belles or a company of solicitors.

How is the party drink *punch* connected to being hit with a fist?

There is no connection at all; the two words look and sound the same but have different ancestry. The punch you drink is named from an ancient Sanskrit Indian word *panca* meaning five, which somehow came to refer to the traditional five ingredients in a punch: alcohol, water or milk, sugar, spice and lemon juice.

To strike forcibly, and usually suddenly, is a variation on pounce.

 What is the background to the word *puttee*?

It's the name for a long strip of fabric that was wound round the leg from ankle to knee and was frequently a part of military uniforms. Apparently the belief was that scorpions and snakes would be able to bite through trousers but not through the puttees. The word comes from India. *Patta* is the Sanskrit word for cloth and that developed into the Hindi word *patti*, from which comes the English word puttee.

(Puttee has nothing to do with putty — the paste for sticking windows in — which derives from the French word *potée*, meaning a full pot.)

 What is the significance of the expression *putty medal*?

Old soldiers use it when someone does something they consider silly. Obviously a good medal would be made of gold or silver, or at least would look like gold or silver. Because they represent ritual significance and long-term prestige, medals usually last a lifetime as a symbol of something done well.

The saying putty medal began as a sarcastic comment on something incompetent, which deserved only a medal made of something transient like putty, which wouldn't last and wouldn't look good — just as the job that earned it wasn't well done.

Over the years the phrase putty medal changed its significance and became a joking way of encouraging someone, maybe a child, more or less commending them for some minor achievement but gently letting them know that there is still some way to go: 'that's worth a putty medal'.

There may be other aspects to the term. In heraldic, or blazonry, terms the shape of the German medal called the Iron Cross is known as a cross patee (from the French for paw — a flattened-out broad-arm cross). During the First World War there was a proliferation of various classes of the Iron Cross so it is possible that the term patee cross or patee medal came to mean something fairly ordinary; there were so many of them that they no longer had great significance.

Is *Qantas* a real word?

It's an acronym, for Queensland And Northern Territory Aerial Services, first registered in 1920.

Where does *quarantine* come from?

Latin originally, but directly from the Italian *quaranta*, meaning 40. A quarantine is a period of isolation for humans or animals to inhibit the spread of existing or possible problems. In early times a quarantine period was 40 days, hence the name. In contemporary times the period of quarantine is adjusted to be the maximum known incubation period of suspected diseases.

Is *Queenstown* one of the many places named after Queen Victoria?

Not directly. In its earliest days, this now busy and prosperous resort town was known simply as 'The Camp'. A.W. Reed's *Dictionary of New Zealand Place Names* allows that the 'popular belief' about the name involves a tiny place in Ireland which Victoria had allowed to be named Queenstown. In the 1860s, there were Irish settlers in the region. One New Year's Day, after the celebrations of the previous night, two rival blacksmiths banged their hammers on an anvil and declared that the little township was to be named Queenstown after the village in Ireland. The 'naming' was mentioned in the *Otago Daily Times* of 6 January 1863.

Does the *quintessence* of something mean there must be five?

It used to. Medieval philosophy believed that everything in the universe was composed of four elements — fire, water, earth and air. But there was a mysterious fifth element of which the celestial bodies were composed, and which was also latent in all things — the quality that could be described as life or love or spirituality. This was the *quint* essence — the fifth element, the invisible force which everything possessed but which couldn't necessarily be seen.

Over time, this term quint essence came to be applied to the essential part of any substance, or an extract that carried the quality which characterised it. The two words joined together and became one — quintessence.

Q **What is a *quorum*?**

The minimum number of people who must be present at a meeting, society, committee or board of directors, before any valid business can be transacted or authoritative decision made. The number varies from one organisation to another, and has usually been ordained when the organisation is established.

Q What have *rabbits* got to do with Easter?

Easter is observed by Christians as commemoration of a death and celebration of a resurrection. The rabbit has more to do with the resurrection than with the death.

When Christianity spread to Europe, there were already a number of centuries-old worship systems in place that couldn't be dislodged and were absorbed and rebranded. Among these were beliefs about the rabbit or, to be strictly accurate, the hare. In ancient Mexico, ancient China and ancient Egypt, various aspects of the hare or rabbit's characteristics were very highly regarded — their speed, their shyness and of course their fertility.

In Europe, the hare and rabbit were widely associated with the coming of spring, because they represented fertility and life. There was an old belief that infertile women could become fertile if they ate hare or rabbit and these creatures were widely believed to have a link with the moon, since the dark patches visible on its surface somewhat resembled leaping rabbits or hares.

The rabbit's fairly obvious liveliness in the fertility department could be seen as representing new life so it came to be incorporated into Christian celebrations of Easter. The image of a rabbit became even more firmly established when retailers discovered that they could sell thousands of toy and chocolate rabbits around Easter time — even if many people had forgotten why rabbits were there at all!

**How can the Scottish expression *ram stam*
be best explained?**

The expression, found in Scottish dialect, means thoughtless, precipitate and reckless. It is also a slang name for a kind of home-brewed beer, possibly because drinking it is inclined to make people giddy and foolish!

There is a relationship with ram jam, meaning stuffed with something, usually food. Stam sometimes occurs as a shortened form of stamp. When the two are put together, the idea arises of something being done forcibly and hastily, such as hastily packing a suitcase rather than carefully and slowly folding everything up neatly.

Q Where does *rant* come from?

In English rant means to rave foolishly. Its ancestor is a Dutch word that came originally from a German word meaning to jump about — to frolic and gambol. The word has been in English a long time and when used by Shakespeare (*Merry Wives of Windsor* — 'I'll rant as well as thou.') and Robbie Burns ('they ranted and sang') it may have been in a transition stage between its meaning of dancing and gambolling and its more recent meaning of loud impassioned talk.

Q Why do you say a person is *rapt* ?

It means totally engrossed, and comes from the Latin *rapere*, to seize. The word was out of fashion for many decades because of its rather poetic image. But in recent times has been taken up by young New Zealanders as a synonym for stoked or chuffed.

Q Why is an unpleasant person called a *ratbag*?

The expression ratbag is believed to have originated in Australia, and is not terribly old. It was first noticed by etymologists in 1910.

The meaning isn't difficult to grasp — an ill-disposed or worthless person, possibly with near-criminal tendencies — but like most pejorative terms it has come to be used by people who are angry simply because they don't like someone.

Semantically it comes into the same category as mortar, in that the qualities of the rat have been transferred to the innocent bag in which the rats are being carried. When you call someone a ratbag, it's not really the qualities of the bag you're talking about.

There was more or less formal acceptance of the term when William Dick's novel *A Bunch of Ratbags* was published in 1965. This may have encouraged the expression into wider use. At a conference in Toronto where on-the-spot translations were being provided, an Australian's reference to some politicians as a pack of ratbags caused total bewilderment among the translators who told their various delegates that the politicians were 'a lot of bags in which rats were being carried'.

Q The headmaster of some boys' schools is called a *rector*. Why?

The word rector comes from the Latin *regere*, to rule. Its relatives can be found in English words like director or regime (a ruling system). A rector can be a cleric in charge of a congregation, a religious house or a college. Gradually the term came to mean a person, qualified cleric or not, who was the head of any school.

Q Why do VIPs get *red carpet treatment*?

Red doesn't signify the only kind of VIP. You can associate purple with royalty, saffron yellow with some Eastern religions, and a high-ranking Roman Catholic like the Pope might be symbolised by white. Various political parties use blue or green. But there is a fairly strong tradition that red indicates importance. And there's no doubt that the use of a red carpet and the phrase roll out the red carpet imply treatment that's either luxurious or respectful or both.

The concept of using a red carpet for important people is very old indeed — it is mentioned by the Greek dramatist Aeschylus in the fifth century BC. And red has consistently cropped up in many contexts where something important is indicated. But the expression red carpet treatment has only gone into general use fairly recently, about 1934.

During the 1930s, there was a train service between New York and Chicago, called The Twentieth Century Limited. The train had only first-class carriages and was famed for its accommodations and its high-class dining. Obviously only rich or important people travelled on it and the entrance to the train, at Chicago station or New York station, was always signified by a strip of red carpet.

 Who originated the saying *Red sky at night, shepherd's delight?*

The most famous speaker of the words was Jesus. He is quoted as saying it in the Book of Matthew, 16:2–3. The usual translation is: 'When it is evening, ye say, It will be fair weather, for the sky is red. And in the morning, It will be foul weather today: for the sky is red and lowring.'

There is a possibility that Jesus was quoting a much older Jewish observation or Israeli proverb, and he would probably have been speaking in Aramaic so whatever he said might have gone through four translations before it reached English.

 What is the background on *red tape?*

British government offices and British lawyers have used a pinky-reddish tape to tie documents into bundles since at least the 17th century. The phrase red tape, symbolising bureaucracy and official stalling, was already in use by the 19th century, and was used by Charles Dickens in *Hard Times* and also by Thomas Carlyle. Both wrote rather bitterly about the slowness of establishment procedures bogged down in paperwork and slow decision making. The shorthand for these processes, according to Dickens and Carlyle, became red tape.

 Where does the expression between a *rock* and a *hard place* come from?

The concept goes back at least to 350 BC when Homer wrote of Scylla and Charybdis, the two evils who guarded the Straits of Messina. Between Scylla and Charybdis came to mean being between two equal difficulties. That progressed into between the devil and the deep blue sea. About 1920 in the United States the old expression about the devil and the blue sea was consciously reworked into a new version about a rock and a hard place.

 A young sportsperson is often described as a *rookie*. What does it mean?

It has been used in the United States since the 1890s to refer to a beginner or a newcomer. The only known origin is that rookie arose as an early mispronunciation of recruit.

Q *Rort* is a very strange word. What does it mean?

The word is used mainly in Australia though it does arise in other places such as South Africa. It can mean boisterous, noisy and rowdy, but the most usual meaning is that someone has set up a system which advantages them at the expense of an existing organisation, or other people.

It has been suggested that the word might be a combination of racket and tort but the *Macquarie Dictionary* doesn't agree. The official definition of rort is 'an incident or series of incidents involving reprehensible or suspect behaviour, especially by officials and politicians', but its derivation, the Macquarie says firmly, is 'uncertain'.

 A street in Charleston on the West Coast of New Zealand is called *Rotten Row*. How did such a name arise?

The street has been called that since about 1865. The most famous Rotten Row is a horse-riding area of Hyde Park in London. During the 1600s it was known as a dangerous area where highwaymen were prone to attack. King William III ordered that 300 lanterns were to be hung, and lit every night to provide more safety, thus making it the first road in England to have night lighting.

Legend would have it that the Plantagenet kings in the 1300s used this road to ride to the royal forests, thus it was referred to as *route du roi*, the king's road, which over time in English became rotten row. There are scholars, however, who dismiss this story as mere folklore. They can only offer instead the notion that the ground underneath was not too firm — it was a rotten road.

This latter explanation may well have applied to a street in Charleston in the 1860s, whether it was named after Hyde Park or not.

 Will the word *royal* vanish if New Zealand changes from a kingdom to a republic?

It will more or less have to, and so will all the other terms associated with it. The word royal comes from the Latin *regalis*, meaning derived from a king or a monarch. The idea that royals are people exalted socially and politically through superior heritage is deeply built into the ordinary consciousness. But if there is no royalty, clearly the word royal loses its meaning altogether. And if the nation becomes a republic, then royal words will have to be eliminated.

So there could be no more royal commisions, just commissions. Eminent practitioners of the law will have to find a replacement for the title Queen's Counsel. The Royal New Zealand Air Force and the Royal New Zealand Ballet will slip back to their plain titles.

Some poor birds — royal albatrosses, royal terns and royal spoonbill — could be in trouble, whether they realise it or not. And there could also be some changes in the arena of public usage: no more monarch butterflies (they might become head of state butterflies) and the entire concept of king-size beds and queen-size beds becomes obsolete. Card players might have to think up a new name instead of royal flush and beekeepers and cosmetics people might drop the first word from royal jelly, which will become just jelly (this could cause confusion in supermarkets).

In fact, changing the words wouldn't change much. Like all the royal words, the president words still mean the person with authority, the ruler.

 How did the word *rugby* originate?

The game could have grown up with a different name. Rugby is the name of an English town and its school. Whether or not William Webb Ellis was the boy who picked up the ball and ran with it at that school (there's a lot of doubt that it *was* him), the town's name lives on in countless clubs, stadiums, changing sheds and millions of television screens.

But the town wasn't always called Rugby. That name developed over the centuries from the town's original name: the *Domesday Book* identified it by the name Rocheberie in the year 1086. Gradually the town's slightly cumbersome name smoothed out from Rocheberie into Rugby. Its famous school began in 1567, generously endowed with estates and a mansion from the bequests of a rich local.

The Rugby school has been rebuilt a couple of times since its inception and William the Conqueror might not recognise its slight change of name since 1086, but almost everyone in the English-speaking world does.

Perhaps it's just as well the town's name changed. You can't imagine Kiwi blokes going out on a Saturday for a game of Rocheberie.

Q | Is *rumpus* an English word?

The word has been known in Britain since the mid-1700s and Somerset Maugham uses it in one of his stories. Unfortunately there are three similar words — rumpus, ruction and ruckus — and all three have mysterious origins.

Ruction is believed to be a shortened form of insurrection, the term entering English speech from the so-called Irish Insurrection in 1798. Insurrection still means the defying of authority, but the shortened version ruction simply means a noisy disturbance or interruption.

Rumpus appears to have originated among 18th-century students in Switzerland speaking Swiss-German and meant then (as now) a lot of noise and activity.

Then there is ruckus, which American scholars say is a combination of rumpus and ruction.

Q | Why was the town of *Russell* given that name?

Before the Treaty of Waitangi, the settlement of Kororareka in Northland had more European people than anywhere else in New Zealand. But the capital of the 'new' country was decreed to be Okiato, a short distance away. In far-off London at that time, the Secretary of State for the Colonies was one Lord John Russell, so in the complimentary fashion of the era, Governor Hobson decreed that the settlement of Okiato be renamed Russell. This lasted for one year, until it was decided that Auckland must be made the capital.

By then the name Russell had become established as a Northland settlement, though its port was still called Kororareka. In time, the name Russell drifted over both places, until in 1844 it was formally decreed that the two places be amalgamated under the one name — Russell. Later, a destructive fire occurred, and Kororareka more or less disappeared.

S

Q **What has *salmonella* to do with salmon?**

Nothing. The bacteria was named in 1900 after an American veterinary surgeon whose work was significant in identifying it: Daniel Elmer Salmon.

Q **Who was *San Fairy Anne*?**

There never was such a person. During the First World War, Englishmen heard French people saying *Ça ne fait rien*, which means it's nothing, it doesn't matter. Understanding the context in which this was being said, the English simply made up a Franglais version, San Fairy Anne, and used it in the same way.

Q **Where does the word *sashay* come from?**

It's a corruption of the French word *chassé*, meaning literally a chasing, a driving away. It became the name of a dance step where the dancer's feet appear to glide. This ballet terminology crept into common usage describing someone who moved as if they were dancing. In English the French word was corrupted to become sashay, and is used to describe walking elaborately, making a self-confident display out of just moving from one place to another.

When a rescue takes place, why do we say someone *saved our bacon*?

The term comes from the days when a household had no refrigerators and bacon was one of the meats that could remain safe to eat during the winter. But the dogs also knew this, and the bacon had to be kept safe from the dogs. Hence the expression saving the bacon became relevant to the important matter of keeping the household larder running efficiently.

But there is also an overlap with the phrase save one's skin, which is an example of synecdoche: mentioning only one part, when you mean the whole thing. To save one's skin is a way of saying that the whole body escaped danger unharmed or was unexpectedly rescued. Similarly, saving the bacon meant saving not just the bacon but all one's food and consequent health. Both expressions have survived but the skin and the bacon have somehow come to mean much the same thing, in that if your bacon has been saved, or your skin has been saved, then you have somehow been rescued and advantaged.

 How did *saveloys* come by their name?

They are a kind of sausage, highly seasoned and smoked, and contain saltpetre which gives them a bright red colour. The name saveloy in English is a corruption of the sausage's French name, which comes from the original Italian name, *cervellato*. That in turn comes from *cervello*, derived from the Latin *cerebellum*, and all of those mean brain. When saveloys were first invented they were made of minced pigs' brains, and their name meant little brains. They might not be made of minced brains nowadays, but that's what the name means.

Why is school called *school*?

The word has a fairly rich ancestry. It began with the Greek word *skhole*, which migrated into the Latin word *schola*. In those ancient times there was a great love of learning and conversation and arguing, and people's time was roughly divided into two activities: work, which was what you had to do to keep everything going, and *schola*, which meant non-working time, when people got together to talk, discuss and learn. The modern concept of non-working time as 'leisure' didn't quite apply: the *schola* time was used to learn. So eventually the word developed the meaning of people gathered together in order to be instructed and to learn. The word went into many other languages, such as Dutch, German, French, and is still there in various forms. The Yiddish version, *shool*, is commonly used to describe the synagogue because that's where people go to learn about the scriptures, the psalms and the laws of living a good life.

Since the development of mass media and labour-saving housing, the connotations of the word school have more or less reversed. In recent centuries children have had to go to school, whether they wanted to or not, and the joys of learning, which used to be a desired activity, face strong competition from the joys of leisure activities and entertainments, which often require less effort.

 What has *scot free* **to do with Scotland?**

Nothing. The expression does not involve Scotland or Scottish people.

In earlier centuries there was an English word, *sceot*, which was originally a Scandiavian word meaning payment. The word was used in English as the name for a kind of British municipal tax, which was levied on people and businesses proportionate to the value of their property, etc. One way of describing the *sceot* tax (slightly inaccurately) would be as a means test. In parts of Britain the tax was in force up to the 1830s.

Some people who should have paid the *sceot* were able to wriggle their way out of it and yet not break the law — what is now called tax avoidance. These people were *sceot* free, and gradually two things happened — the pronunciation changed to scot and the term came to mean someone getting away with doubtful behaviour and not being in any way held responsible.

Q How is it that *Scotland Yard* isn't in Scotland?

Before the death of Elizabeth I in 1603 Scotland and England had separate monarchies. But then, when James VI of Scotland (James I of England) took over both thrones the position of monarch was resolved into one person and has remained so ever since. But when there were kings and queens of Scotland, there were ambassadors from Scotland to England, and sometimes the Scottish king or queen would come to visit London. On such occasions all these dignitaries stayed in a sort of palace in one part of the city. The town square where this palace stood became known as Great Scotland Yard.

Over 200 years later, when the headquarters of the Metropolitan Police were established in 1829 in Whitehall, the entrance to the police establishment opened into Great Scotland Yard. Gradually the name of the city square was shortened to Scotland Yard, and that became a shorthand way of saying the police. Even the term Scotland Yard became shortened as well: often it was just the Yard.

In 1890 the police administration shifted to another address, christened New Scotland Yard. Another shift came in 1967, but the name of Scotland Yard had by then become fixed in people's minds.

Q What on earth are the *screaming abdabs*?

They started out as the habdabs, which was a slang term for the bits at the end of a meal. Things like dessert and maybe cheese or nuts — those were the habdabs. During the Second World

War the military took up the word and it lost its h and became the abdabs, which gradually moved from the food to the drink, and was used about people who'd drunk too much. The term moved into more serious vein when it came to mean *delirium tremens*.

Later, screaming was added and the expression came to mean any period of intense frustration or confused exhaustion.

 Q Does the nursery rhyme *See-saw Marjory Daw* have anything to do with sawing wood?

Yes. Two-man cross-cut saws and pit saws were manufactured at least as early as 1622 and possibly earlier. At more or less the same time — the 1600s — a little ditty came to light, which usually goes:

See-saw Marjory Daw,
Jacky shall have a new master,
Jacky shall have but a penny a day,
Because he can't work any faster.

In those days the song was not a nursery rhyme or a children's song, but was chanted by builders, specifically two men using one saw, to help them maintain their to-and-fro rhythm and thus work efficiently.

There was also a slightly ribald undertone to the words, because during the 17th century Marjory Daw was a slang term for a woman of easy virtue, so the to-and-fro rhythm had another significance for the men who were singing it and doubtless kept them cheerful.

The song gradually spread and eventually became adopted by children, who weren't using a cross-cut saw but were playing on a see-saw. The song (and the word see-saw) moved from working sawyers into children's playgrounds.

When did the word *segue* moved away from music into general use?

The word is Italian — *segue* means now follows. It is written on one section of a piece of music which is intended to follow on immediately after the previous section finishes. About the middle of the 20th century the term began to be used in a slightly different context, but still about music, when radio announcers would announce that two separate records were coming up, and that they would segue. This meant that the records would follow each other, without any talk in between. According to traditional usage, this was not 100 per cent accurate because the two records were *different* pieces of music.

But it did make sense, and by the 1970s use of the expression had extended from radio people announcing records into general usage: to move from one topic or event to another seamlessly and smoothly.

 If the words *September, October, November and December* actually mean 7, 8, 9, 10, why do they denote 9, 10, 11 and 12 in our calendar?

Our calendar has an immensely complex history. We now enjoy a fairly stable 365 days divided into 12 months with seven-day weeks and a leap year every four years. It wasn't always like that. The calendar as we know it has had three major overhauls: first the Roman Republican calendar, followed by the Julian calendar, then the Gregorian calendar.

In ancient Roman times, what we call a year used to begin in March. This was partly because before that time of year it was too cold for armies to set out to war, but the weather started easing up a bit then so the month was named after Mars the god of war. The armies were able to march and the year's activities began.

In those days there were 10 months. After March came April, named for Aphrodite, goddess of love and beauty. Then May honoured Maia, goddess of spring. June was believed to be named in honour of the influential Junius family — and by happy coincidence the first day of that month was already dedicated to Juno, goddess of marriage and women's well-being. Quintillus and Sextilus were the fifth and sixth months, followed by September, October, November and December.

But various upheavals occurred. Ancient Romans were very keen on commemorating celebrities, so Mark Antony renamed the month of Quintillus and called it July — to commemorate Julius Caesar. Similarly the month of Sextilus was renamed to commemorate the emperor Augustus.

In 1582 Pope Gregory made a stern effort to tidy up the year's calendar, which was beginning to wander all over the place. And somewhere during the calendar revisions, the beginning of the year was changed to honour the god Janus who faces two ways and guards entrances and exits, and he became January. There was also an ancient sacrificial event when maidens lined up and were slapped with a piece of goat-skin called a *februa* in the belief that this would keep them virginal and help them to be fertile — later on. This festival became the name of another month, February.

But in shifting the year's official starting point two months earlier, it was somehow overlooked that there were now 12 months in the year, and that the last four of them were named with words that meant seven, eight, nine and ten.

And we're stuck with it.

Q **What does the *serpent and the elephant* mean?**

It's a phrase used by Charles Dickens in *Hard Times* and refers to the visible signs of the Industrial Revolution. The serpent is the smoke spiralling from big industrial chimneys, and the elephant is the steam engine. On other occasions Dickens, with heavy irony, described the enormous factories that grew around the English countryside as fairy palaces, because when their windows were lit at night they looked like real palaces. But in the daylight the illusion was destroyed.

Q Where does the expression *seventh heaven* come from?

The answer to this is quite straightforward but the background is not. We need to examine both words: seven and heaven.

Versions of the word heaven have been in the English language for centuries, dating back to the Old English *heofan* and there are similar versions in Dutch — *hemel* — and in German — *Himmel*. The word has developed various other connotations since its use in biblical texts, for the Bible doesn't paint any clear picture of heaven (although hints can be found that there could be divisions in heaven).

There are poetic references to afterlife but no concrete description of heaven and the Jewish concept in the Bible is that the exact nature of the immortality of the soul is known only to God. Another interpretation of the Jewish concept is not that people are in heaven but that heaven is in people. As Christianity developed it generated different connotations based on interpretations of translations of the Jewish concept of heaven as mentioned by Jesus, who was Jewish.

Nowadays, according to the *Oxford Dictionary of Christianity*, the usual definition of the word heaven is based on the distinctive hope of followers of Christianity that the faithful will rise after death and join Jesus there.

But there are other meanings of heaven. Centuries ago astronomers were aware that there must be something beyond the visible sky, and although they didn't use the words outer space, that is essentially what they meant. Quite unbowed by the fact that they had never been beyond the sky and probably thought nobody ever would, those ancient scientists divided their concept of space into plural heavens. That wording still remains with us, in expressions like the heavens, meaning the vast areas of space.

So now let's look at the word seven.

It seems quite ordinary. But for many centuries the figure seven has had a mystical resonance. The Pythagoreans noted that it comprised four plus three, both lucky numbers, so seven was treated as mystic. Ancient peoples in Babylon and Egypt revered seven sacred planets. The Jewish concept of the seven-day week is now more or less universal, and from that developed the concept of sabbatical leave after seven years work, and also the Jewish concept of jubilee — seven times seven years plus one = 50 years.

We are aware of the seven virtues and the seven deadly sins, and a belief that the seventh child of a seventh child is of special interest. Ancient alchemists worked with seven metals; the Japanese have seven gods of luck.

Christians have divided the life of the Virgin Mary into seven joys and seven sorrows, and their church services may contain seven sacraments. The ancients spoke of the seven wonders of the world.

Even natural features like the seven hills of Rome and the Seven Seas of the world add to the special qualities that surround seven. Jesuits believed that the first seven years of a child's life fashioned its thoughts for ever. Pillars of wisdom come in sevens, the most famous samurais were a magnificent seven and the ancient German folktale gives Snow White seven companions. Legend tells us that the Babylonian goddess Isthtar rescued the soul of her dead husband by travelling to the underworld, which had seven gates, and at each gate the price of admission was that she shed one of her seven cloaks or veils. (This shedding of seven veils resurfaces in the Bible in the story about Salome.) Shakespeare divided man's life into seven ages and a type of rugby game has seven people in each team. There is even a natural phenomenon called the seven-year itch.

Clearly, then, placing the word seven alongside the word heaven is combining two words that both carry a lot of luggage.

The term seventh heaven as we use it comes from the Muslim religion. Among the detailed beliefs of some divisions of the Muslims, there is a belief that heaven is the place of the afterlife. But unlike the Jewish heaven, which is inside people, or the Christian heaven, which is a mystical place you go to after death, the Muslim heaven can be described in great detail, and is subject to distinctions of rank, class and depth of earthly faith.

Here they are:

Heaven No. 1 is made of silver, and is inhabited by angels who hang glowing lamps on chains — hence we have stars.

No. 2 is made of gold.

No. 3 is made of pearl and contains huge books that contain the names of the newly born, while the names of the newly dead are diligently blotted out.

No. 4 is made of white gold, and the angel of tears lives there, weeping endlessly for the sins of mankind.

No. 5 is made of both silver and fire, where the avenging angel presides.

No. 6 is made of rubies and garnets, and that's where the guardian angel of heaven and hell lives, made half of fire and half of snow.

No. 7, made of divine light, is beyond the power of the tongue to describe. Those who live there are each larger than the whole planet of Earth, each inhabitant has 70,000 heads, each head with 70,000 mouths, each mouth speaking 70,000 languages. All the inhabitants and their tongues are forever employed chanting the praises of the Most High.

Clearly Heaven No. 7 is very big indeed (and very noisy). But the inhabitants must also be very, very happy, because that's what the expression means. If you're faithful enough and lucky enough to have passed through the gold and the silver, the snow and the fire, the garnets and the rubies, and reached the final level, then it is a kind of ecstasy. You are in seventh heaven.

Q What is the origin of the word *shampoo*?

It comes from India. A Hindustani word, *champo*, means to knead or press, and originally a shampoo meant a massage. Somehow it moved upwards to mean the head only and then became a slippery cleansing substance for the hair. But it really means to rub around. Most words that came into English from India retained much of the original meaning — curry, jodhpurs, calico, pyjamas, bungalow, chutney, dungarees, verandah. But shampoo took a more narrow road and instead of applying to the whole body, narrowed itself down to just the head.

What is the difference between a *shanty town* and a *sea shanty*?

The two words sound the same but they have different ancestry. The French word *chanson* (a song, from *chanter*, to sing) became the ancestor of the term sea shanty.

But the shanty in a shanty town is a different word altogether. It comes through Canada, from a different French word *gantier*, which means a supporting framework. *Gantier* eventually gave rise to two English words: gantry which is a supporting framework in building and engineering projects, and shanty, which is a rather rough living structure. Neither a gantry nor a shanty is known for its fine detail.

 Is there any reason why the word *she* is so often used for non-female concepts?

This occurs in the classic phrase she'll be right and terms like she's a great little car or she's really turning out to be a beaut day.

The concept isn't new. For a long time things without a gender have nevertheless been given one — sometimes without any logic. For centuries the moon has frequently been referred to as she. The ocean and rivers are often called she and ships have been she since ancient times when it was believed that various separate gods were assigned to look after various separate things — and the god which hovered over and cared for a ship was invariably female. Various sections of the Christian church are customarily referred to as she or mother, even when the ruling hierarchy is entirely male.

So, though there's no logical reason in many cases, there's ample precedent for assigning a female gender where no gender exists. The *New Shorter Oxford Dictionary* explains that she has developed a meaning of 'it', or the state of affairs, as in she's jake. Australian and New Zealand men have embraced this use with particular fervour and often replace the word it with she.

Q **What is the origin of the rebuke** *she's the cat's mother*?

The expression seems to carry some sort of hint that anyone referring to someone else as she has been rude, though it isn't clear why. There is a resistance in what we call 'polished society' to overuse the word she. This comes mainly from other women, usually mothers, and the phrase developed during the 19th century as a reproof addressed to children who constantly said she instead of a person's name. This applied particularly if anyone said she about a woman who was in the room at the time. No valid reason can be put forward, though there is a frail belief that saying she has a faint echo of she-cat about it.

Q **Is there a word for people who collect** *shells*?

The Latin for spiral-shaped or snail-like is *cochlea* and is connected to the Greek word *konkhe*, which gives us the English word conch, a spiral mollusc. The term also occurs when describing other things that are naturally curled or twisted such as part of the human inner ear, which is called the cochlea. Thus, the word cochlearists is a fairly logical word for collectors of shells.

Q **How did the expression** *shoot my bolt* **arise?**

It means to do everything to the limit of your power and even slightly beyond, to exhaust your current possibilities. The term, which has been in use since at least 1200, comes from archery.

The crossbow was the heavy artillery of ancient warfare, and the crossbow shot a very heavy arrow called the bolt. The tension needed to do this was such that the crossbow had to be wound up with a windlass. Sometimes in the heat of battle when time was of the essence the crossbow archer had only one chance to shoot his bolt. The retensioning of the bow took so long to set up again that he could take no further part in immediate action. He had shot his bolt!

Q In the song *'Shortnin' Bread'* what is actually being sung about?

It doesn't mean what we would call shortbread or even bread. The song is believed to be a genuine slave song that originated among the plantation slaves in America, and was used as a lullaby. It was first published in 1915 but is much older than that. The word short is often used as an abbreviated version of shortcrust and describes a kind of dough or pastry that crumbles easily when it's been cooked. And shortening can mean any kind of cooking fat. There is a vague rule that short dough has half the quantity of fat to flour.

In plantation times shortnin' bread was made after a pig-kill, with half the quantity of fat to cornmeal (not flour) containing bits and scraps of bacon, and served with bacon gravy. Black American slave talk also had its own double meanings: shortnin' bread was also another phrase for intimate activity.

Q What is meant by the term *silvertails*?

The word is used in several different ways — it's a kind of cat, a kind of plant, and the name of a sports team — but since about 1900 it has had a slang meaning referring to a rich person, a swell, a toff. And from there it's developed a side connotation of social climbing, being affected.

Q Why are some women called *slappers*?

The word has been used in North England dialect since the late 1700s, where it referred to a big person, usually clumsy and usually female. The word drifted into more common usage during later centuries, and it gained some connotations in the early 20th century from a quite different expression — slap-and-tickle, meaning sexual foreplay. The phrase often implied that a woman was quite forthcoming in allowing this.

Originally the expression had no shade of impropriety. It described someone like Norah Batty on *Last of the Summer Wine* who is definitely female and definitely does not allow slap-and-tickle, but is cumbersome rather than graceful in her movements. This would be a true use of the word slapper in its original sense.

But a more recent connotation has a slapper as less like Norah Batty and more like Bet Lynch on *Coronation Street* — fairly big in build, brassy with it and not so young any more.

Another shade of meaning has also crept in because a good-time woman often overdoes the slap (make-up).

Q **Is *smithering* rain related to *smithereens*?**

They're both dialect words, which can make connection difficult to trace. Smithering is very fine rain. Smithereen comes from an old Irish word *smidrin*, meaning small pieces. This word was sometimes abbreviated to smithers and sometimes expanded to smithareening, which seems believably close to smithering.

Q **How did we get the term *snake oil*?**

The manufacture of what are usually called patent medicines began in England and they were being licensed by the early 1700s. Considerable quantities were shipped to America, but this exporting stopped when the Revolutionary War started there.

Entrepreneurial Americans moved very quickly to fill the gap, and during the 1800s there abounded a large supply of so-called medicines to cure all manner of complaints. There was Enriched Vegetable Compound, Swamp Root Kidney and Liver Medicine, Kikapoo Indian Cures, Seminole Cough Balm, Celery Compounds, Great Sulphur Nostrum and a bottled cure for cholera that was widely used by missionaries to deal with anything among the heathen from corns to toothache. Also available was an ointment to cure baldness and another to develop the bust. A man called Sutherland had seven daughters with long hair — a total of nearly 11 metres of hair. He made a mixture called Seven Sutherland Sisters Hair Growth Tonic.

Amidst all this, there was a definite belief that extract of snake could help some medical problems. There actually were people who killed snakes and extracted their secretions and it was widely believed that the native Americans used grease from rattlesnakes to alleviate the pain of rheumatism. Some very brave travelling medicine men actually stood on public platforms while they killed the snakes and squeezed their juice into the medicine. So naturally a whole host of medicines began to appear which purported to contain genuine snake oil.

However as science advanced and gullibility retreated, it was gradually revealed that many of the bottles supposedly containing snake-oil cures actually had only a mixture of turpentine, camphor, beef fat and some ground up red pepper, which imparted a slight warm sting to the skin.

So the term snake-oil salesman began to gain disrepute, and when the American Federal Pure Food and Drug Act came into effect in 1907 the phoney remedies were curtailed. But reference to snake oil remained, indicating 'medicine' of very doubtful value.

There are genuine medicinal qualities to be found in some snakes: the Chinese water snake is a source of an enzyme that helps decrease blood pressure and the Malayan viper produces heparin, which is a blood anti-coagulant. But these treatments are not available off the backs of trucks.

 Milton's poem 'At a Solemn Music' uses the phrase *solemn jubilee*. **How can a jubilee be solemn?**

Solemn has shades of meaning: serious and sincere, but also with pomp and ceremony, inspiring awe. Milton was writing in the 1600s when all these shades of meaning were still current with jubilee, which doesn't necessarily have to be all gaiety and fireworks. There are various ways of showing respect and joy.

Q **Is there a connection between a *spanker* and *spanking*?**

The name of a fore and aft sail placed in the aftermost part of a sailing ship is a spanker — in full, referred to as the spanker mast. There is no clear reason why it's named this way, but the word spank does have a subsidiary meaning of being fast (as in a spanking pace) so there is a possible relationship between the name of the spanker and the ship's speed.

The other spank was defined in 1727 as to slap with the open hand. The word is thought to be imitative, named for the noise it makes.

There appears to be no connection between the sail spanker and the word spank meaning to slap.

 Q **Although it has come into computer language, *spam* used to mean some kind of meat. What kind of meat?**

In 1936 the Hormel Food Co. launched a competition to find a name for a canned meat product. Apparently the company didn't want to call it pork loaf (though that's what it was) and was not permitted to call it ham because the meat was shoulder, rather than hindquarter. A prize of $100 was awarded to a New York radio announcer who suggested Spam, a condensed version of spiced ham. Later, in 1970, the Monty Python crew performed a ludicrous television sketch in which a run-down café served only many variations of Spam, the customers' indignation climaxing in a ridiculous song called 'Spam'. This contributed greatly to the word becoming widely known, even when the commodity itself wasn't.

Brewer's Dictionary of Modern Phrase and Fable credits the Monty Python sketch with the use of the word spam to mean unwanted e-mail material which arrives relentlessly.

Q **From where do we get the expression** *spin doctor*?

Most people can talk and most people can throw a ball. But in high level sports, some people learn to throw a ball very skilfully and by giving it a clever spin they can fool people about the exact path the ball is going to follow. In ball-throwing sports, the term spin doctor arose to describe such people.

Gradually the term moved away from sports, and since the 1980s has been used to describe people who control information. They put a favourable spin on certain announcements.

Q **What does** *splice the mainbrace* **actually mean?**

The term dates back to sailing ship days, when the heaviest piece of running rigging was called the mainbrace. The job of splicing this mainbrace was difficult and tiring. When the job was done, the reward for all who took part was an extra ration of rum. There is still a descendant of that custom, even in non-sailing ships. When a ship's company deserves special congratulations, or on ceremonial occasions such as when a new monarch succeeds to the throne, the order is given to splice the mainbrace — and extra grog is served. In non-nautical life, the term has come to mean simply let's have a drink.

Q **Was there a real person called** *Spooner*?

Indeed yes. The Reverend William Spooner (1844–1930) was Warden of New College, Oxford and had an endearing habit of absent-mindedly muddling the initial letters of successive words. This aberration is now named after him — spoonerisms. Some of the howlers attributed to him were: The Lord is a shoving leopard, the cat popped on its drawers, a half-warmed fish, a blushing crow and a well-boiled icicle.

How does the word *spondulicks* come to mean money?

The term was first noticed in the mid-1800s and although it is widely used in the United States, it is believed to have begun in London. The origin, however, is unknown. The word may simply have been made up. But there is a noticeable similarity to the Greek word *spondylicos*, which in ancient times was a special kind of seashell used as currency instead of coins. The two words are so much alike that it's quite possible spondulicks comes from *spondylikos*. What is hard to explain is how a word from ancient Greece suddenly leapt back into use in the middle of the 19th century.

 A commentator referred to PM Helen Clark as a *Stakhanovite*. What is it?

The term Stakhanovite dates from 1935 when a Russian coal miner called Alexei Stakhanov produced more loads of coal than his fellow workers, by means of rationalisation, and so far exceeded the compulsory daily requirement that he was given a special reward. This began a system called Stakhanovism, which was the Soviet name for 'raising production by offering incentives to efficient and enthusiastic workers'. The word crept into English to refer to an exceptionally hard-working person whose dedication and productivity are beyond the norm.

Why do so many countries' names end with *stan*?

The suffix stan is derived from the Farsi language *ustan* or *istan*, meaning state or country. Many centuries ago, the Persian Empire stretched geographically over an enormous area, and its official language was Farsi. Established areas within the empire were known as a *stan*, meaning a state. The sense was roughly similar to that in which the word state is used in the United States of America, whereby each state is an almost autonomous area, but still under the ultimate governorship of a federal government.

Eventually some of the Persian Empire's states became completely independent countries, but many of them retained the old Farsi word *stan* in their name, even when the people no longer spoke the language. Since then there has been a slight shift of emphasis in the meaning of the word and stan has come to mean country or the land of.

Turkestan, land of the Turks

Tadjikistan, the wreathed people's land (they wear turbans)

Uzbekistan, land where the Uzbek language is spoken

Afghanistan, land of Afghan, the legendary forefather of the Afghan people

Baluchistan, the land of the Baluchs — the 'tufted hair people'

Kazakhstan, land of the Kazak (the 'free men')

Luristan, land of the Lurs tribe.

Pakistan resulted from the partition of India. The new name of this country was first proposed in 1931 and established in 1947, although its precise meaning is not clear. The Urdu word *paki* can mean people pure in spirit. But the name is also believed to represent the initial letters of Muslim states — Punjab, Afghanistan, Kashmir, Iran — plus stan.

Q How did *Stewart Island* get its name?

New Zealand's 'third island' has had various names. In pre-European days it was referred to by its Maori name of Rakiura, which means glowing skies. When the island caught Captain Cook's attention he decided to call it Solander Island, commemorating a well-known botanist of the time. Cook changed his mind, and the island became (briefly) New Leinster. But an Invercargill-based official loved the place so much that people began to call it after him — Pearson's Paradise.

Lurking in the wings was William Stewart, who made the chart of the island for Captain Cook. Eventually the island's name was settled on as Stewart Island and its inclusion as officially part of

New Zealand was clarified by Governor Hobson sending a flag to
raise over it in June 1840.

When did the saying A *stitch in time saves nine* **begin?**

If a thread is loose, it is better to mend it straight away
before the weakness allows other threads to become loose and
serious repair is required. The saying was first seen in print in
1732. Gradually, over a long time, the expression moved away
from sewing but retained a relevant meaning. If you see something
going wrong that you could fix up right now, then it's best to do
something about it as soon as you notice it.

**How does being in a drugged state
get to be called** *stoned*?

The term is believed to have originated among jazz musicians
and originally it was stoned out, meaning drunk. By the 1940s it
had assumed a secondary meaning of being drugged, especially
on marijuana, which, unlike heavier drugs, leaves a person still
able to talk and think and reason, albeit in a euphoric state.

History is silent about exactly why the word stoned was used to
describe this state. A guess would be that the person in the drunk
or drugged state was behaving as if they'd been hit over the head
with a stone.

What is the background to the expression
straight-laced?

There is sometimes a spelling mix-up here (like bated breath)
because strictly the expression should be *strait*-laced, strait meaning
narrow, tight, restricted (e.g. he was in dire straits, or straits used
for a narrow strip of water).

From the middle of the 16th century onwards, the expression

strait-laced was used to described someone who was obstinate, uncommunicative, rigid, scrupulous.

Because of similarity to the image of a woman wearing very tight corsetry and therefore having a straight back, the spelling is often seen as straight (which still fits with the original meaning). In more recent times the original meaning has shifted slightly from desisting from things criminal to an indication of conventional, honest, and conforming to social pressures.

Q **What is the difference between *student* and *pupil*?**

There has never been a firm clarification of this — or at least not one which matches general usage. The generally perceived difference between those two words was that (a) a pupil was one who was taught by a teacher, and attended formal lessons during which the teaching took place and (b) a student was one who studied — and might go to some classes and receive some guidance but was expected to absorb a deal of learning by working alone. The separation was simple: children were pupils until they left secondary school and then became students at tertiary university level.

But a tendency to aggrandisement caused a gradual change during the 1970s and 1980s so that the word pupil vanished quietly and rapidly and all schoolchildren were referred to as students.

An interesting sidelight can be observed in news reports involving a school-aged child: if the child has done something good, it is usually referred to as a student, but if it is involved in something bad, the term pupil is often used.

Q **What does *subfusc* mean?**

It isn't a word heard very much in non-university life. *Fuscus* is Latin for dark and *sub* means below. Thus the English word subfusc means very dark indeed.

In some universities subfusc means academic dress, usually a capacious black gown. The word is quite common in those circles and even appears on invitations to indicate that academic gowns are to be worn.

 Q **Were the early *suffragettes* so named because of their suffering?**

No, the word suffragette has nothing to do with suffering. It comes from the ancient Latin *suffragio*, meaning broken pieces, usually crockery and pottery. Paper wasn't common in those times, so people voted by laying a piece of broken pottery, *suffragio*, onto one named pile or another. Hence suffrage — the right to vote.

In 1881, some women could vote in the Isle of Man, which became the first country to allow women to vote. New Zealand women who campaigned for the suffrage right were called suffragettes (in some other places they were called suffragists). Eventually they won their battle in 1893 and New Zealand (which was a colony, not an independent country) followed the Isle of Man and surpassed it, by making the parliamentary vote available to all adult women. England did not permit women a parliamentary vote until 1918.

Q **Why do people say *sure as eggs*?**

The popular version is actually an abbreviation, being a shortened form of sure as eggs is eggs. The term has been in use since at least the mid-1800s: you'll find it in the operetta *Cox and Box* (1867) and later in Agatha Christie's *The Mysterious Affair at Styles* (1920).

But the expression actually comes from quite a different source which has nothing to do with eggs. It traces back to a mathematical statement that sounds similar: X is X, which means that X exists and is a certainty. Over time the saying X is X became corrupted to sure as eggs is eggs (meaning the same thing — a certainty) and eventually to just sure as eggs.

Q Does *swear like a trooper* mean soldiers?

Yes, but it isn't quite fair. The expression arose in the 18th century, when soldiers lived quite differently from their 21st-century counterparts. Most 18th-century soldiers were not educated, their social position was more clearly defined (and was bound to be fairly low on the scale) and they were not the focus of vibrant television recruiting commercials and media interviews. In other words, the non-fighting behaviour of the 18th-century solider was less exposed to public scrutiny.

So we shouldn't judge 18th-century soldiers because they swore a lot in a tough all-male environment. Though the expression still exists and is frequently used, it doesn't necessarily imply that men are any better or worse if they swear profusely in an all-male environment.

Actually, when the expression is used, it is usually said about someone who *isn't* a soldier, which carries a subtle connotation that though it's okay for soldiers to swear, hearing it from someone else is unexpected — *they* are the ones earning disapproval, not the soldiers. But the origin of the expression is easy to see: to swear like a trooper means to break into profanity as frequently and pungently as an 18th-century soldier.

Q Are *swells* just big waves?

Absolutely not. But there is sometimes confusion between the two. Mariners don't always agree about what properly constitutes a swell, but in general it is recognised to be a state caused by wind which generates heaving within a defined area, resulting in a group of waves which break only when they reach shallower water (hence surf). But until that point, the swell is mainly under the surface of the sea and may or may not be visible. A swell (singular) can be the cause of waves (plural).

A particular swell is formally designated by its height and the direction of the wind that produces it. It would be rare to find two different swells in one fairly small place (e.g. when a radio reporter says 'there are big swells in Lyttelton Harbour,' he probably means there are big waves in Lyttelton Harbour — but caused by just one swell.).

It is possible that a westerly swell could occur at the same time as a southerly swell (in open sea, not a harbour). If they did not cancel each other out, the result could be very unpleasant indeed.

A basic rule for landlubbers: waves (plural) are caused by a swell (singular), so if you see waves, no matter how big, call them waves, not swells.

How did the expression *taking the piss* arise?

It means to make fun of and reduce pomposity by deflating a person's self-importance. In full the expression would be taking the piss out of someone. When a person badly needs to go to the loo, and then is able to, they have been deflated (albeit willingly). When you make fun of someone pompous, you are, figuratively, deflating them — unwillingly.

Q *Talkback radio* **seems to dominate the airwaves. When did it start in New Zealand?**

It began in 1927, on National Radio, when topics such as possible war with Japan, tobacco prices and the meaning of the word Bolshevik were discussed with listeners.

Talkback radio means that the listening public can talk back to the announcer (usually by phone). Those talking back are not like interviewees who have been invited to speak — anyone from anywhere can join in and say what they think about the topic being discussed.

Since the invention of telephones and radio, there has been a careful distinction between that which is spoken on a telephone being private, and that which is spoken on a radio being public. Anyone who decides to phone a radio station cannot be said to be having their privacy invaded.

Q What is the origin of the tune 'Taps' as used at the end of the day by Scouts and Guides?

Bugles or wind instruments have been used for military signals over many centuries. Horn calls were used during biblical times, during the Roman Empire and in practically every battle since. These various calls and signals customarily include one that marks the end of the day — either the day's fighting, or the end of recreation after the fighting.

The British military has signalled the end of the day with a bugle tune called 'The Last Post' since the 19th century, and still do. It is also often played at funerals.

The American military had a slightly different set of calls, and up until 1862 they customarily used a French tune which was called, in rough translation, 'Put out the fires' to end the day. But the Americans referred to this tune by the word taps, actually a shortened version of the Dutch word *taptoe*, which signalled the closing off of barrels of beer, etc., because the soldiers had to stop relaxing and return to the garrison. (That Dutch word *taptoe* eventually became what we call a tattoo — a ceremonial return to barracks.)

In 1862 General Daniel Butterfield decided that the usual tattoo, or taps bugle call, was too formal. Calling in a bugler named Oliver Norton, he hummed bits and pieces of bugle calls he knew and between them they cobbled together an entirely new tune. Butterfield could neither read nor write music but he was an experienced military man, he knew all the signals well and he was able to dictate what he wanted. The tune was used that night. It never had a name — it was simply called 'Taps', and it was so effective that it quickly spread throughout the Civil War and was officially adopted by the United States Army in 1874. Because of the way the tune goes, the soldiers began to call it the Go-to-sleep call, or the Put-out-lights call. Six different versions of words have been written to the tune.

The British concept of Scouting became very strong in the United States and the American taps song gravitated towards the American Scout movement. The Cubs movement in New Zealand took on the American taps song for the end of the day and it gradually spread throughout the country. It received a boost during the Second World War and eventually became standard for Kiwi Scouts and Guides.

A word of caution: people sometimes think the British 'Last Post' bugle call and the American 'Taps' are the same thing. Not so. There is a similarity in the tune, but they are entirely different pieces of music with different histories.

Q When did the word *teenager* become common?

The suffix teen is derived from ten. The British etymologist, John Ayto, is convinced that the word teen was in use in England in the 17th century, as a noun, usually used in such phrases as in one's teens. By 1894 this use had moved to the United States — as teen or teener. Then there's rather a gap until the phrase teen age girls was first seen in 1921. From then on both teen age and teen-age were seen (as adjectives), and then the noun teenager developed, which went into use around the late 1930s.

Q Where does *tell the truth and shame the devil* come from?

The term can be found in various versions from 1548, and it was acknowledged at that time as being a fairly familiar phrase so clearly it is older.

You'll find it in Shakespeare's *Henry IV Part I* — 'Tell truth, and shame the devil!' — written about 1597. Ben Jonson used it in his comedy *A Tale of a Tub* in 1633 and John Fletcher in his play *Wit Without Money*, written in 1639. The shape of the expression seems to have remained more or less unaltered since then.

When was the term *terrorist* coined and what does it mean?

The word is originally French — *terroriste* — and has been in use since the late 1700s. During the French Revolution in 1789 there were people who believed that violence and bloodshed were necessary methods for propagating their own principles of political supremacy. They were referred to as *terroristes*.

Over 200 years later, the meaning hasn't changed much, but the weapons of warfare have advanced considerably. The word means the same thing as it did in the 18th century, but terrorism in the 21st century brings much greater violence to far more people in a much shorter time.

It is virtually impossible to formally define terrorism, but one attempt would be: using and favouring violent and intimidating methods in order to coerce a government or community.

The big difficulty with the word terrorist is that your definition depends which side you're on — an event interpreted as severe coercion by the people it affects would probably be described by its instigators as a liberating blow for freedom.

How long has there been a *Third World*?

There was, and still is, only one known world. But in April 1952 French economist Alfred Sauvy started the expression Third World on a comparable basis to the expression Third Estate at the time of the French Revolution.

Three years later in 1955 there was a conference of 29 African and Asian nations in the town of Bandung in Indonesia. During that conference, the French diplomat Georges Balandier referred specifically to those 29 nations as the Third World. The term was reported, it quickly took on and has since broadened in meaning to include any underdeveloped nations.

At that time the 'numbered worlds' were understood to be:

First World — the so-called Western bloc of democratic fully developed countries,

Second World — the Communist bloc,
Third World — the 'developing' countries,
Fourth World — countries capable of development but have not yet done so,
Fifth World — countries for which there is little hope.
Time caught up with the above designations and Third World is the only one still heard.

The term developing countries is seen as a more polite way of saying undeveloped countries. *Brewer's Dictionary of Twentieth Century Phrase and Fable* describes developing countries as: those with insufficient agricultural and industrial productive capacity to generate the savings required to sustain investment and economic growth. Common features include dependence on the export of primary products, widespread poverty and disease, and illiteracy.

 Some official documents use the word *timeously*. What does it mean?

It's a Scottish word that means sufficiently early. For instance, if your street is going to be dug and pipes laid, the council will notify you about traffic disruption, etc. that will last until the work is completed on date X — if the weather allows the work to finish timeously.

 How did the term *tin-canning* come into being?

Tin-canning was sometimes called tin-kettling and was a very common ritual well into the 20th century, particularly in rural districts. It isn't so easy to organise in cities. The tin-canning happened sometime after a young couple married. If they went to their house to begin married life on the spot, so to speak, friends and neighbours all gathered late at night, carrying buckets and baby baths and tins filled with stones and sticks to hit things with. They made a great deal of loud noise, marching in circles around the house if that was possible.

Or if the couple went away on a honeymoon, the noisy visit would happen on the first night that they came back. This practice was not at all uncommon throughout New Zealand from approximately the 1860s to the 1960s.

Villagers gathering together and bashing tins, etc. is a very old British custom, but it originally signified extreme disapproval. If someone in the village had done something unkind but not illegal — if, say, a wife or husband was known to be unfaithful — the neighbours would have no hesitation in gathering round the house at night and making a noise to express their displeasure. It is the origin of the expression ran-tan, which was originally ran-dan, and meant everyone gathering together and making a big noise in order to humiliate a person who couldn't actually be legally charged with doing something wrong.

Somewhere between Britain and New Zealand, the mechanics of the tin-canning ritual remained exactly the same as they had been for centuries, but the intent became reversed. In a weird kind of way the tin-canning was intended as a welcoming gesture, an expression of goodwill.

 Is there any actual thing which is called a *tittle*?

Yes. It has come to mean a very small amount, deriving from a term used in printing as early as the 1600s, and possibly before. The word can be found in the King James version of the Book of Matthew 5:18.

In printing, a tittle refers to a tiny piece of print like the dot over the letter i and the little additions that are made to the tops and bottoms of some letters to influence their pronunciation (such as in Spanish). These are also sometimes called diacritics.

Tittle was sometimes used by people who wanted to compare a situation with something detailed and exact. There's a line from a Beaumont and Fletcher play: 'I'll quote him to a tittle', meaning that everything will be exact, every tiny dot in place.

What is the origin of the expression *to a T*?

The most widely believed explanation is that the expression comes from the T-square used by architects and draughtsmen. This is used to draw absolutely accurate angles, parallels, etc. and so the connotation has carried over to other areas — to a T means as if drawn with a T-square, therefore exact.

This explanation has been disputed on the grounds that the expression is in fact older than the term T-square and comes from the fuller saying to a tittle. A tittle is a tiny stroke in printing (see previous entry) and saying to a tittle meant that standards of exactness were being applied. Over time the saying became shorter, as just 'to a T'.

Was the soldier *Tommy Atkins* a real person?

No. The 'name' comes from a document given out to all people who enlisted in the British Army from about 1815. The recruits were given an introductory booklet containing several forms that had to be filled in. To clarify how the forms were to be filled in, there was a sample copy with things already filled in. The sample document, in the space where it said 'Recruit's name', had a printed made-up name: Tommy Atkins. From that false name Tommy Atkins quickly became used to apply to all British soldiers.

This is somewhat reminiscent of a British pop group whose members had had some bad patches on the dole so when they formed a rock group they named it after the number on the top of the official government unemployment register form — UB40.

What gave rise to the farewell phrase *toodle-pip*?

There have been several variations on this way of saying goodbye: toodle-oo, tooraloo, tottle-oo, toodle-pip and just toodle by itself. There are two explanations, one rather more believable than the other.

Some scholars have a theory that toodle-oo is an English imitation of the French goodbye phrase *tout à l'heure*, meaning see you soon. But there is no solid evidence for that. The other explanation is based around the old English word toddle. In the 18th century, the word meant stroll away, leave.

Nowadays we use it mainly to describe a baby learning to walk, but the old meaning of walking away occasionally still survives — you'll hear someone say I must toddle now.

The development from toddle into toodle-oo or tootle-oo was just a sort of comic extension. Toodle-pip and tootle-pip developed more recently, with a suffix borrowed from the radio signal announcing the hour.

 What on earth are *tranklements*?

This is an English dialect word which is quite well known in the area from which it comes — the Black Country, roughly between Birmingham and Wolverhampton. People from that district are well acquainted with tranklements, which simply means small possessions, bits and pieces of household paraphernalia. Although the word isn't widely used outside that area, an Irish band has called itself The Tranklements, possibly just because it's an attractive sounding word.

U

Q How did *Ulan Bator* get its name?

It is the capital of Mongolia and the name commemorates the eminent Mongolian Dandimy Sühbaatar (1893–1923), who was responsible for founding the modern republic of Mongolia. He was known as the red warrior. Hence *ulan* meaning red, and *bator* meaning warrior.

Q Where does the word *umpire* come from?

Originally from France, but its history is moderately complex. The original French word was *noumpere*, applied more to legal situations, where an impartial arbitrator for a dispute was required. *Noumpere* meant not a peer — peer in the sense of an equal. The arbitrator could not be associated in any way with either party in the dispute. The word found its way into English (with the same meaning) during the 14th century.

Gradually two things happened. First, a process called metanalysis took place, where a letter from one word migrates across a space to a neighbouring word. Hence a noumpere slowly became an oumpere and then an umpire (similarly a napron became an apron. See also **nickname**). And second, the word and the practice of its arbitration, moved mainly (but not entirely) towards the upholding of rules and decision in sporting situations.

Q Was there ever a real *Uncle Sam*?

Apparently yes. A man called Sam Wilson was born in the United States in 1766. He became experienced in the meat industry and was hired by the US Army to inspect the meat bought by them. Most of his fellow workers addressed him as Uncle Sam.

There was a war in the States during 1812 and Uncle Sam Wilson either supplied meat to the army or inspected meat they had already bought — it's not quite clear — but either way, when he declared the meat to be acceptable, he put his initials on the barrels, and because everyone called him Uncle Sam he wrote 'US', not 'SW'. When people assumed that the initials stood for the United States, they were told that it stood for Uncle Sam.

By 1852 there were cartoons depicting this benign old man, and gradually the phrase Uncle Sam came to signify the nation or government of America.

Uncle Sam Wilson was known to be a man of great fairness, reliability and honesty, and those who knew him took very kindly to his being associated with the image of all Americans. He died in 1854, and his grave is in Troy, New York, where he lived. There is a statue of him in that town commemorating him as the original Uncle Sam. In 1961 the American Congress declared that Samuel Wilson was the inspiration for the symbolism of the Legend of Uncle Sam.

Q Why is the person arranging a funeral called an *undertaker*?

Almost every form of society has rituals, legal formalities and tribal customs surrounding death. And there are also practical matters —a body, a grave, a venue, a death certificate and so on. Coping with all this can be very traumatic for those who are closely connected with the deceased.

Up to the 1600s, the term undertaker was applied to anyone who was undertaking an organisational task. It was a sort of title that included functionaries in the political and magisterial arena, and also the people who supervised after-death matters. The term gradually slipped away from all the other people and undertaker remained in use only in the funeral context.

 Which abbreviation is correct: *USA*, or *US* — *without the A*?

The abbreviation US has been in evidence since at least 1818. The use of the abbreviation US links up with the cartoon figure called Uncle Sam to symbolise America in general and the government in particular. (See **Uncle Sam**)

Hiram Ulysses Grant, whose mother's maiden name was Simpson, was accidentally enrolled at military school as Ulysses Simpson Grant, which change he kept. He became president and the initials US gave him a symbolic link to the figure of Uncle Sam.

There was also a period when the dollar sign had two perpendicular lines running through it instead of one. American patriots joined up the two lines at the bottom, so it made U over the top of S — another way of promoting the name of the country. That didn't survive, but shows that abbreviating has been going on for a long time.

Note that the United States of America isn't the only nation state that begins with US: its neighbour Mexico is properly entitled the United States of Mexico. It seems, though, that custom and usage has found a solution, at least among English speakers. When people mean the United States of Mexico they simply say Mexico, and when they mean the United States of America they simply say America.

It would seem, therefore, that of the three abbreviations, US of A is hardly ever used, and both the others — USA and US — are acceptable, with a slight preference towards USA in formal circumstances.

Q Why do we *vent our spleen*?

In ancient times various organs were regarded as the 'seat' of certain emotions. (This mindset survives in the way the heart, for instance, is still regarded as a source of affection and love.) The humble spleen is a fairly obscure internal organ, seldom mentioned. But it was thought to be the seat of a person's ill humour, bad temper and mirth. Over the centuries the mirth somehow became forgotten and outbursts of bad temper were described as the spleen being vented (from the Latin *ventus*, meaning wind).

Q Where did the word *Velcro* come from?

Switzerland. In 1948 Swiss mountaineer George de Mestral became annoyed at the prickly burrs of mountain bushes, which clung to his clothes and to his dog. He decided to try turning the plants' pesky characteristic into an advantage for himself, so approached textile experts who might be able to reproduce the hooks on seeds which would then cling to any fabric with a loopy surface.

Only one weaver in France managed to do it. He made two strips, one with hooks, the other with a loopy surface, and he took them to the Swiss mountaineer. They called it hooked locking tape. It took until 1955 for the invention to be patented, by which time George de Mestral had dreamed up a name: *vel* from the first part of *velour* (French for velvet) and *cro* from the first part of *crochet* (French for a little hook). Thus, Velcro. Where would we be without it?

Q What is a *vested interest*?

Most of the various meanings of vest originate in the Latin *vestis*, meaning clothing. One meaning of vest (when followed by in or with) concerns the conferring of authority: 'with the power vested in me by . . .' or 'the executive was vested with the authority to . . .' Following that track, the word vested became a legal term meaning to have an established right to something (e.g. property). The term is often used informally to describe a situation where it is to someone's definite advantage that a project succeeds — they have a vested interest in its success and may make a personal profit.

Q How did computers come to get *viruses*?

There used to be 'germs' in New Zealand and all school-children were warned by posters, lessons and admonitions about the dangers of Bertie Germ — a cartoon figure who was depicted as lurking in grimy places and waiting to leap onto hands not properly washed. Then scientists discovered the virus, which was much smaller, and quickly became very fashionable. Being 'down with a virus' sounded much more trendy than 'sick with a germ' and the word germ all but faded from consciousness.

In 1972 a science-fiction writer, David Gerrold, dreamed up a story about a weird computer glitch which not only disabled computers but was able to replicate itself. He called the aberration a virus. The matter achieved a much higher profile in 1983 when a real American scientist, Fred Cohen, demonstrated a development that was very close to the fictional one. At the time, a colleague named Lane Adelman suggested that if this mishap should ever happen, it would be like a virus. It did happen. A computer disruption developed which did exactly as fiction had predicted — it could disable an electronic system, replicate itself and infect its surroundings to devastating effect. It was called a computer virus. Within 10 years of the expression first being heard, the problem had become so common that it hardly needed the word computer in front of it — just virus would do.

How long have we had the word *Walkman*?

Since 1979. The founder of Sony, Masura Ibuka, was a frequent traveller and wanted to listen to music while travelling but not to bother other people. At his request, Sony technicians developed a small battery-operated radio and cassette player which used headphones, and with which you could walk around. It owed some features to an existing cassette player called Pressman, and with that product's name in mind, plus the popularity of Superman, the Sony team registered the name Walkman. Like many other trade names, Walkman gradually became part of the normal language.

Since 1979 there have been 200 different models of the device. Later models included the facility to play compact discs. Nobody other than Sony can use the name Walkman, so other firms bringing out other versions had to invent similar (but different) names. And note that the plural is Walkmans, not Walkmen!

Q **Some of the words now used to report *war* are not easy to understand. What do they mean?**

Military terms are among the trickiest to keep track of: firstly, the methods of fighting battles have changed radically over a short period of time, so the language we become accustomed to during one period quickly becomes obsolete as the military comes up with new inventions, if not new words.

Secondly, a huge political spin is often put on words being used to report war, because the authorities have decided that we, the public, must gain a certain impression of the progress of the conflict. Hence, people listening to radio reports or reading newspapers find words and terms being used which do not abide by their dictionary definitions. This can result in a certain vagueness.

War: This word is subject to constant pressure. In fully formal terms the word means the existence of declared armed conflict between one nation state and another. According to that definition, there never was a war between the United States and North Vietnam, no formal war with the Falklands Islands, and the 2001–02 situation between the United States and Afghanistan was not actually a war because no formal declaration was made by one nation state to another.

However the dictionaries have had to admit that the word war has been used so often outside that formal context that nowadays you'll find it means open, armed conflict between two or more parties.

For instance, the New Zealand Land Wars are customarily referred to as wars. They did not involve two nation states, but they were certainly armed conflict between two or more groups.

Asymmetrical warfare: This incorporates the word asymmetric in its sense of being unequal or unbalanced. Asymmetrical warfare is a term that has been used by the military for some time. In the past it referred to a situation where a small group with ardent beliefs attempted to attack or terrorise a much larger group, for example terrorists pitting themselves against an organised nation state.

These days the term is being used with a slightly different connotation. Asymmetrical war seems sometimes to describe a state of conflict, but *not* one between two nation states. No country has actually made a formal declaration of war against another country.

Taken out: This is a soft-soap way of saying caused maximum killing, chaos and destruction.

Ground zero: this term used to relate to either the exact area where a bomb hit the earth, or the point of detonation of a fixed device. But the term has undergone a change. No bomb was dropped on the New York World Trade Centre towers on

September 11, but the damage to them and to the ground around them was as if a bomb had dropped. So you'll hear ground zero being used now to designate the area damaged because of an attack of some kind.

Ethnic cleansing: This is a particularly euphemistic expression, meaning genocide. Because it deliberately contains the word cleansing there seems to be something pure and attractive about the activity, but it actually means to deliberately kill all people of a certain ethnic group.

Collateral damage: This began as a euphemistic description of the number of civilian people actually killed in a military attack. Instead of saying 'Hundreds of civilians were killed', someone will say 'There was collateral damage'. Besides dead bodies the expression can now include upheavals of other kinds caused by an attack: airline policies, insurance problems, the sharemarket, the tourist industry, etc.

 Where did the phrase *wash your dirty linen in public* originate?

It can't be established that Napoleon actually invented it, but in 1815 he certainly said it — or a near-equivalent. Translated, Napoleon's line was, 'It is in the family, not in public, that we wash our dirty linen.'

 What actually happened at *Watergate*?

Watergate was originally a name from Britain (found for instance as the name of a theatre in Villiers Street, London). The name apparently inspired an American builder, who gave the same name to a big complex of flats and offices in Washington. Some office suites in the Watergate building were occupied by the headquarters of the Democratic Party. During the 1972 American elections the Republicans tried (illegally) to bug the communications of the Democrats. This was apprehended and then the incident was covered up. The eventual disclosure of the whole story, by two Washington journalists, resulted in serious charges of corruption and eventually led to the resignation of President Richard Nixon in 1974.

Since then whenever there's been a seemingly simple incident which actually leads to revelations of corruption or disruption of the status quo, journalists have enjoyed finding the core-word of the situation then adding 'gate' to it, so we get Paintergate, Dianagate, Corngate and so on.

 When was a dominant woman first described as *wearing the pants*?

Pants used to be called breeches, so the expression has been in use since 1600, originally as 'She wears the breeches'.

 What is the origin of the term *wedding breakfast*?

The basic meaning of the word breakfast is to break a fast — to eat after you haven't eaten for some time before. In modern usage breakfast by itself has come to mean the first meal of the day when you haven't eaten anything since dinner the night before, but at other times in history the word was used to mean any meal at all when you hadn't eaten for a while beforehand. Shakespeare used it in this sense.

It is human nature to have a social gathering after an important ritual event — university graduation, a homecoming, a burial, a major sports match, a marriage. Within the British heritage, the Christian rituals associated with a marriage have slowly been added to or incorporated into the rituals of pre-Christian times. When Christianity in Britain was younger, a couple who declared themselves committed to each other only went to the church for a blessing, after the event. Gradually, however, the commitment ceremony itself moved towards being held at the church, although not inside it. There was an initial reluctance about a Christian priest announcing inside a church that a man and woman were now officially allowed to sleep together.

So marriage blessings or marriage ceremonies, when presided over by priests, were usually conducted on the steps outside the church, and after this, the gathered guests would all move into the church and take part in a mass. That's the clue — because it was once the rule that people did not eat before participating in a mass. Hence, after the ceremony, and the mass that followed it, the bridal couple and the guests would literally break their fast.

In recent times the word breakfast has been used less frequently. Marriages take place at various times of day and are not all Christian services. Hindus, Jews, Buddhists, Sikhs, etc. have different marriage customs, nearly all of which involve an after-ceremony celebration of some kind, but general usage now calls this a reception rather than a breakfast.

Q Where does the word *week* come from?

The Jewish concept of a constant cycle of seven successive days is generally known as a week. Going way back to ancient Greece, the word *taxis* had a connotation of speed and things being efficiently organised. This gave rise to the East German/Scandinavian gothic word *wiko*, meaning order, and that was the ancestor of the German word *Woche*, meaning a week. *Wiko* also drifted into Old English to name a succession of seven days, gradually evolving from words such as *wice*, *wicu* into week.

Alongside this were the two expressions *feowertiene nihte* and *seofan nihte*. One of those vanished in English and both of them vanished in the United States. *Feowertiene nihte* become fortnight (never used by Americans) and *seofan nihte* was modified into se'en night, meaning a week, but its use simply died out, and the older word became the standard term in English.

Was the name *Wendy* invented especially for *Peter Pan*?

J. M. Barrie's character of the boy who wouldn't grow up was first seen in the 1904 play *Peter Pan*. The book, *Peter and Wendy*, was published in 1911. Barrie can't be credited with inventing the name Wendy but he certainly popularised it. A legend has grown that Barrie was inspired to use the name because of his friendship with a little girl called Margaret Henley who died when she was only six. Little Margaret used to call Barrie her 'friendy' but couldn't pronounce it properly so it came out 'fwendy', or 'fwendy-wendy' in some versions of the story.

There were, however, people called Wendy before the Peter Pan story. The name may possibly be derived from Gwendolyn and it can be found in British and US Census statistics throughout the 1800s. In ancient times there were also at least two Emperors of China called Wendi, though one feels that their connection with Peter Pan would have been slight . . .

Was there ever a *wigwam for a goose's bridle*?

No, never. Not even when it turned up (as it occasionally does) as a whim wham for a goose's bridle. The phrase means nothing, it has no defined origin, it isn't a cover-up for anything else. It's just an amusing invented nonsense phrase which indicates that something is foolish, impossible or private — and people say it when they don't want to explain whatever they're being asked about.

What is or was a *whipper-snapper*?

The term is usually used by a person of maturity about someone else who is younger — and inexperienced and possibly even impertinent. It has been used in the United States more frequently than in Britain, though it originates in England as far back as the 1600s and its history is strange.

In the 1600s snipper-snapper described young people who were fond of cheeky remarks and repartee and crisp patter. This earned such people a reputation of being foolish wasters of time and not very effective. Nowadays we would call them lippy, or smart-mouths. Round about the same time there developed a custom among young men who were known as ne'er-do-wells (which was the 17th-century way of saying hoon) to stand on street corners, idly flicking a whip just to pass the time. They were referred to as whip snappers.

Over the years a gentle amalgamation of the terms took place and snipper-snappers and whip-snappers became combined into whipper-snappers.

 Why do people say *white rabbits* on the first day of the month?

For many centuries, mankind has been intrigued with the mystery of animals, and people have developed dozens of suspicions and beliefs about such creatures as cats, dogs and rabbits. Almost all of these beliefs have no basis in fact; they stem from some sort of desire to link attractive animals more closely to humans.

Saying white rabbits on the first of the month is linked into beliefs so old that there is no single answer to why people believe that saying it will bring good luck. Over the centuries, dozens of semi-supernatural things have been believed about rabbits and hares. Here is a selection:

- If a rabbit or hare crosses your path in front of you it is good luck, though the quality of the luck varies depending on whether the rabbit is going right to left, or left to right.
- If a rabbit crosses your path behind you, that's bad luck (though it isn't clear how you would know that a rabbit had crossed behind you).
- If a rabbit runs through your yard you will have children.
- Hares are actually witches in a physical form — keep away from them.

- Hares contain the spirits of dead grandmothers, so be nice to them and never eat them.
- It is very bad luck to shoot a black rabbit.
- If you dream about rabbits then misfortune will visit you.
- Many people believe a rabbit's hind feet touch the ground before its front feet do, so power, speed and luck are associated with the hind foot of a rabbit. If you carry one, you will have more power, speed, luck and fertility — like rabbits.
- If you ever lose your rabbit's foot, your luck will turn bad.
- If the rabbit's foot is taken from a rabbit killed during the full moon by a cross-eyed person, it will bring exceptionally good luck.

Most of those things mentioned are associated with British superstition, going right back to the belief that Queen Boadicea used rabbits to help her plan the route her army would take. But there are many other rabbit stories in other cultures — Mexican, Korean, Aztec, Buddhist. Buddha created a calendar system from the 12 creatures gathered around him, one of which was a rabbit.

Now somewhere in the middle of this a belief arose that mentioning rabbits on the first day of the month brought good luck for that month. Unfortunately, like many old superstitions, there is no definitive statement about exactly who said so, or exactly what to do. Even the day is in question. One version of the superstition is that you must say this on the first day of the new moon (not necessarily on the first day of the calendar month).

In addition to that confusion, there is more confusion about what you must actually say. A selection:
- You must say white rabbits once.
- You say white rabbits three times.
- You say just rabbits once — or three times (no need for the 'white').
- Contemporary America has produced two variations — wabbits (which is 'white rabbits' condensed) or — bunny bunny bunny.

Those who argue for the use of white rabbits rather than just rabbits, point out that there is an established association of white with purity, and also that white rabbits are quite rare.

To add to the confusion, there is dispute about exactly when you say it and to whom:

- You must say it out loud first thing on the first of the month before you speak any other word.
- It must be spoken before your feet touch the ground.
- It won't work unless you say it to someone on the first of the month and you must say it before they say it to you. The person who says it first gets the luck, the other one doesn't.
- Here's a killer — saying white rabbits first thing in the morning doesn't work unless you said black rabbits last thing the night before.

My advice is just to forget the whole thing.

 How is it that you never know *when your number is up*?

It's an old expression that is believed to have originated in the navy. When someone died and his place in the dining room was empty the other men said he had lost the number of his mess. This resurfaced as an expression in the US Army — a soldier who has been killed is said to have lost his mess number.

Hence when your number is up had a connection with death. It is used rather more widely now, indicating that you will be required to account for your responsibility, or that something you dread will happen but, as with death, advance warning is unlikely.

Q **Why does something give you the *willies*?**

It's a feeling of discomfort and nervousness. This expression arose in the United States towards the end of the 1800s but it's now fairly universal through the English-speaking world. There are two theories about the origin. One is that it is related to an old expression the woollies, which refers to the itchy sensation on the skin when wearing wool (and we're talking 19th-century wool here, not fine-weave).

The other theory is more interesting. In 1835 the German writer Heinrich Heine published a book called *From Germany*, which included reference to folklore belief from the Slavic countries about *wilis*. These are wood-nymphs, the spirits of maidens who have died with a broken heart, usually because they were jilted. The young women are found in the Serbian and Croatian languages as *vila*.

Besides Heinrich Heine's book, the Slavic legend received two other major boosts into worldwide recognition. One was the ballet *Giselle* in 1841 (directly based on Heine's story), which has an entire *corps de ballet* of *willis*, and then in 1905 came Franz Lehar's operetta *Merry Widow* in which the leading lady, the widow, who is a Slav from Montenegro, sings a song about a *vila* — a witch of the wood (which in the English translation comes out as *vilia*).

The song and the ballet took the words *vilia/wilis* and the concept right round the world and brought increased recognition of the words into the English language. And because they were eerie ethereal creatures, people feeling creepy about something said they had the willies.

So, two possible explanations, one about woolly underwear and the other about beautiful forest ghost-women. You may choose.

Q **How is it that *woebegone* seems to mean woe is not gone?**

The word seems to be telling woe to be gone, which seems to mean that sadness is being ordered to go away. But there is a deception in that word begone. Usually it means go away but what we have in this case is a much older word, absolutely archaic — *begon*, meaning to be beset with, surrounded by. Thus came the saying *me is woe begon* — which means woe is besetting me, surrounding me, is attacking me.

Over the years the four-word expression contracted to one word, woebegone.

Where are *Wolfenstein* and *Castle Wolfenstein*?

Inside a computer game. They're not real places, but a generated game with a manufactured Gothic vocabulary and a horde of devotees who do clever things on computers in which they fight imaginary creatures and take unto themselves imaginary glory.

The name is very likely a play on Mary Shelley's famous novel of 1818 about a young doctor called Frankenstein, who created a monster by assembling various human parts. Near Eberstadt in Germany you can still visit the real 15th-century Castle Frankenstein, in which the Frankenstein family lived.

 Is *Worcestershire sauce* from Worcestershire?

Yes and no. Lord Marcus Sandys enjoyed a certain sauce in India, and brought the recipe back from India to Worcestershire in 1834. He gave it to the local chemists, Mr Lea and Mr Perrins, asking them to make it. Everyone hated the result, but forgetfully left it in the cellar. Three years later someone walking past saw it, and bravely decided to taste the strange three-year-old mixture of salted anchovies, garlic, cloves, onions, tamarind and chillies. Behold! They had accidentally done what the Indian cooks forgot to tell Lord Sandys — left it to mellow. A marvellous rich, dark liquid was now available.

Oceans of it have been used since, especially since Americans took to it in 1874 and later used untold quantities in Bloody Marys.

Americans insist on calling the sauce by its full name — 'Worcest-er-shire' — when nearly everyone else, including New Zealand, refers to it as 'Wooster' (as in Bertie). And some places in New Zealand call it simply black sauce.

Q   What is a *wowser*?

There have always been people who declined to drink any alcohol. Those who did partake often made put-down remarks about those who didn't, and one of the sneer terms was wowser — a person who drank no alcohol and thus by implication was a kill-joy and a dullard. The word is based on the old English dialect word *wow* meaning to complain. There is a certain logic in that, since those who did not drink were inclined to mention that they disapproved of those who did. So it is not a surprise that the word wowser gathered a quite strong pejorative connotation.

Current fashion shows signs of reversing the situation, encouraging people not to drink too much, especially if driving. The person driving-but-not-drinking is seen as sensible rather than a wowser. So the word has practically disappeared from use.

X

Q **Does the word *Xerox* mean anything?**

Yes. The particular copying process it describes was invented by Chester Carlson in 1937 and was originally called electrophotography. In 1952 his company registered the word Xerox as its trade name, derived from the Greek *xero* meaning dry.

Q **Is it disrespectful to write *Xmas* instead of Christmas?**

Not at all. In ancient Greece the letter *chi* was written with a symbol very like a modern X. Thus the word Christ (a title assigned to Jesus by worshippers, meaning the annointed one) was written as Xristos. This was frequently abbreviated to just X. So if long precedence brings respectability, then writing Christ's Mass as Xmas has been considered acceptable for over 1000 years.

Q **How does a *xylophone* get its name?**

A real xylophone is made of wood. Small tablets of wood are placed in a row and each makes a different tone when hit with a hammer. It is named from the Greek *xylo* meaning wood and *phone* meaning voice or sound. Hence xylophone means sounds made from wood.

How did the word *Yankee* come into being?

There has been dispute about this for years, resulting in sixteen different versions of the word's origin. There are two main theories:

(1) That American native peoples, coming to terms with early European settlers, attempted to say the word English, which came out as *Yengeese*, eventually becoming Yankee.

(2) Dutch settlers in New York used a derisive name, Jan Kaas (John Cheese), to refer to English colonists in Connecticut, and that deteriorated into Yankees. (A secondary version of that same story is exactly the opposite: that the derisive name Jan Kaas was not said *by* the Dutch settlers, but was said *about* them.)

 Does *yeah right* simply mean yes?

Partially. The effect of the phrase depends somewhat on the way it is said (paralanguage — the conveying of information by the tone within the voice, rather than the words). Although the words are supposedly agreeing with whatever statement came before, saying yeah right implies that a person does not in fact agree at all and is calling the previous statement into question. Superficially the phrase yeah right appears to be a confirmation, but has become a form of vocal irony.

Which is correct, *You've got another think coming*, or another *thing*?

The original expression was, 'If you think that, you've got another think coming.' It may have evolved from another expression which said, 'You've another guess coming', but certainly early in the 20th century people were saying 'You've got another think coming' as a folksy piece of advice, never intended to be grammatical, just an amusing way of saying, 'You're wrong.'

Somehow an alternative version arose: You've got another thing coming.

That version sprang to prominence during the 1980s in a hit recording by the British heavy metal band called Judas Priest — who made a record actually called 'You've Got Another Thing Coming'. Segments of the recording went on to be used as the sound-track for TV commercials about hamburgers. This gave the phrase enormous coverage and now there are people firmly wedded to both think and thing.

 What is the signficance of the *yule log* at Christmas?

Many of the customs and activities associated with Christmas have nothing to do with the birth of Jesus and the yule log is one of them.

Christianity absorbed all kinds of rituals that were associated with deep, dark winter. For many centuries, countries with terribly cold winters held a midwinter festival in December, which served to establish that the cold months were halfway through, and therefore the warmer months were now on their way. A festival of 12 days evolved, based on the belief that the three Magi came to see Jesus 12 days after he was born.

In English, the word yule has an ancient and mysterious ancestry. Some believe it to be a Norse word for wheel; others are convinced that yule is a surviving form of one of the 200 names for the powerful Norse god Odin (as in *yölfödr*). Either way, in Scandinavian countries the term yule became the general name for the whole 12-day Christmas festival. A big log was chopped down, then set alight to honour the sun and to symbolise the light and warmth that would come when winter was over.

This custom filtered through to England in the 11th century and was gradually adapted into the Christian festivities because December was chosen as the month in which the birth of Jesus would be celebrated.

Some special customs grew up around the yule log. It must never be bought — to be really effective, the yule log had to be a gift from someone. Little doughy figures were baked sitting along the log in the fire — and they eventually became gingerbread men. The wassail bowl would be drunk, indicating goodwill and good health for everyone — and that survives as what we now call Christmas drinks.

It was believed that good luck would come to the house if the log remained burning for 12 days. Besides which it was a holiday for servants for each day that the log kept burning. (Hence the gossipy legend that in the middle of the night servants would creep down to the log and dab water on it to make it smoulder and burn more slowly.)

But after 12 days it had to go. It isn't entirely clear why. The only explanation offered that having 12 days of festivity represented the hope that 12 happy months would follow. So on the 12th day the yule log went, but a small piece of it was kept, to be used as the lighting-up-stick for the next year's yule log.

Obviously the custom of burning yule logs or any sort of logs was more feasible for rural people. But a feeling of attachment to the custom was so strong that people moving to city areas wanted to keep the tradition alive, so they invented a substitute. The substitute yule log was a dark brown sponge, formed into a roll and covered in chocolate icing. Thus was born the chocolate log!

Where does the word *zany* come from?

Italian. The original Italian word was *zanni*, which served two purposes. It was a diminutive for the name Giovanni (John), but also meant a silly fool. The latter use crept into English, slightly softened in application, to mean something or someone pleasantly funny and whimsical.

 What is the background to *zap*?

The word was invented in 1929 by Philip Nowlan, the creator of the comic strip character Buck Rogers. The word was short, didn't take up much space in a cartoon frame and its unusual aspect lent itself to bold and dramatic borders on the speech balloons. It usually indicated either a quick movement or a telling strike (from something like a ray gun). Quite quickly zap went into the language and developed various other shades of meaning: to bombard with protest, to speed through television commercials, to effect an electric shock, even to kill. It has also become a noun indicating energy and power — 'He shows a lot of zap.'

Q **In an interview *Xena* actress Lucy Lawless mentioned the *Zeitgeist*. What does that mean?**

The word is a combination of two German words: *Zeit*, meaning time or period of time, and *Geist*, meaning spirit. Together, as Zeitgeist, they mean the prevailing spirit, attitude or general outlook of a specific time period, as reflected in its literature, art, politics and philosophy. Ms Lawless may well have been explaining that *Xena* somehow satisfied the Zeitgeist of the time in which the television show aired, when audiences seemed to accept and even desire elements of fantasy, as later proven by the overwhelming success of *Harry Potter* and *The Lord of the Rings*.

Q **How did we get the word *zero*?**

It comes into English from the medieval Latin *zephirum*, which is derived from the Arabic word *sifr*, which means empty.

Q **What is the connection between a *zip* that closes things up and a *zip code*?**

There is very little connection. The zip that closes things up was invented in 1893 by American engineer Whitcomb Judson, who referred to it as a clasp-locker, and then as a universal fastener. Later it was called a hookless fastening and a C-Curity. Initially the device had problems and went through several developments before 1921, when the Goodrich company started using an improved version on galoshes. The company named these overshoes Zippers, thought to be because of the noise the fastener made as it was closed. The name of the shoes became transferred to the fastening that closed them, and the world gained zippers (often shortened to zips).

Over 40 years later, the US Postal Service began a process of refining people's addresses to include a group of numbers that would speed mail district identification, and thus delivery. Beginning in 1963, the number system was called a Zone Improvement Plan code — zip code for short. It is believed that the postal authorities deliberately planned the process's name so that it would give the impression of enhanced speed, and zips — having proved quicker than buttons — certainly carried that connotation. This is the only connection between the two uses of the word zip.

Q The late Freddie Mercury was described as a Zoroastrian. What is that?

Rock star Freddie Mercury was born of Iranian (Persian) parents and his real name was Farouk Bolsara. The family's religion was Parsee, based on the teachings of the ancient philosopher Zoroastra.

Zoroastra (also known as Zarathustra) dates back to Persia in 1200 BC when he became the centre of and prophet for a religion fostering belief in a single God. The German writer Friedrich Nietzsche examined the ancient teachings in his work *Also Sprach Zarathustra* (pub. 1883–1892), which caught the attention of composer Richard Strauss, whose later tone poem of the same name (1896) was known in English as *Thus Spake Zarathustra*. Apart from Freddie Mercury's death and Zoroastrian funeral, the biggest previous publicity Zoroastra had in the Western world was the use of Strauss's music for the 1968 movie *2001 — a Space Odyssey*.

Q What is *zydeco*?

It is black cajun music indigenous to south-west Louisiana and west Texas, and is derived from old French and African-American idioms from the mid-19th century onwards. The origin of the unusual name zydeco has been widely disputed — but is generally believed to have arisen from a mispronunciation of the French phrase *les haricots ne sont pas salé* (the beans have no salt) — an idiom indication poverty.

Zydeco music, which combines elements of cajun, rock, Caribbean, rhythm, blues, funk and hip-hop, is constantly changing form, depending upon the band. Most of the music isn't written (or at least published) so the same song played by two different bands will sound different. Instruments playing the music usually include the piano accordion, saxophone and sometimes the fiddle, with washboard percussion and sometimes drums and electric bass.

Bibliography

The following works of reference were consulted in answering the questions in this book:

Ayto, J., *Twentieth Century Words*,
 Oxford University Press, Oxford, 1999.
Beeching, C., *A Dictionary of Eponyms*, 2nd Edition,
 Clive Bingley Ltd, London, 1983.
Benét, W. R., *The Reader's Encyclopaedia*, 2nd Edition,
 Adam and Charles Black, London, 1965.
Biedermann, H., *Dictionary of Symbolism*,
 Ware/Wordsworth, UK, 1996.
Boyd, L. M., *Boyd's Book of Odd Facts*,
 Signet Books (Sterling Publ.), New York, 1980.
Brasch, R., *A Bee in Your Bonnet*,
 Angus & Robertson/HarperCollins, Sydney, 2001.
Brasch, R., *How Did It Begin?* 2nd Edition,
 Collins Australia, Sydney, 1985.
Brasch, R., *There's a Reason for Everything!*
 Fontana/Collins, Australia, 1982.
Brewer, E. C., *Brewer's Dictionary of Phrase & Fable*, 15th Edition,
 revised by Adrian Room, Cassell, London, 1996.
Brown, L. (ed.), *The New Shorter Oxford English Dictionary*,
 Clarendon Press/OUP, Oxford, 1993.
Burnham, T., *More Misinformation*,
 Ballantine Books, New York, 1981.
Burnham, T., *The Dictionary of Misinformation*,
 Ballantine Books, New York, 1976.
Chapman, R. L., *American Slang*, 2nd Edition,
 Harper Perennial, New York, 1998.
Claiborne, R., *Loose Cannons, Red Herrings*,
 W. W. Norton & Company, New York, 1988.
Cross, F. L., *The Oxford Dictionary of the Christian Church*,
 Oxford University Press, Oxford, 1985.
Dunkling, L., *Dictionary of Curious Phrases*,
 HarperCollins, Glasgow, 1998.
Ehresmann, J. M., *A Pocket Dictionary of Art Terms*,
 John Murray, London, 1980.

Encyclopaedia Britannica, 15th edition
(30 vol), Hemingway Benton/Britannica, Chicago, 1979.

Flavell, L. and R., *Dictionary of Idioms*,
Kyle Cathie, London, 2000.

Funk, C., *A Hog On Ice*,
Harper Resource/Quill, New York, 2001.

Funk, C., *Heavens to Betsy*,
HarperPerennial, New York, 1993.

Funk, C., *Thereby Hangs a Tale*,
Harper Resource/Quill, New York, 2002.

Gordon, I., *A Word in Your Ear*,
Heinemann Educational, Auckland, 1980.

Gordon, I., *Take My Word For It*,
Wilson & Horton, Auckland, 1997.

Hendrickson, R., *Encyclopaedia of Words & Phrase Origins*,
MacMillan Reference Books, New York, 1987.

Jones, A., *The Wordsworth Dictionary of Saints*,
Wordsworth Editions, Ware, 1994.

Levy, J., *Really Useful*,
Quintet/New Burlington, London, 2002.

Lock Stock and Barrel!
Past Times, Oxford, 1998.

Manser, M., *The Guiness Book of Words*,
Guild Publishing/ Guiness, Enfield, 1998.

Manser, M. H., *The Wordsworth Dictionary of Eponyms*,
Sphere Books, Ware, 1988.

May, J., *Curious Facts*,
Seker and Warburg, London, 1981.

Orsman, H., *The Dictionary of New Zealand English*,
Oxford University Press, Oxford/Auckland, 1997.

Oxford Dictionary of Quotations,
Guild/Oxford University Press, Oxford, 1985.

Panati, C., *Extraordinary Origins of Everyday Things*,
Harper & Row, New York, 1987.

Partridge, E., *Dictionary of Catch-Phrases*,
Routledge & Kegan Paul, London, 1977.

Partridge, E., *Dictionary of Forces' Slang*,
Seker & Warburg, London, 1948.

Partridge, E., *Dictionary of Slang and Unconventional English*, 7th Edition,
Routledge & Kegan Paul, London, 1970.

Partridge, E., *Origins — A short Etymological Dictionary*, 4th Edition,
    Book Club Associates (& Kegan Paul), London, 1966.
Pickering, Isaacs, Martin, *Brewer's Twentieth Century Phrase and Fable*,
    Cassell, London, 1991.
Reed, A. W., *The Reed Dictionary of New Zealand Place Names*,
    Reed Books, Auckland, 2002.
Rees, N., *Cassell's Dictionary of Clichés*,
    Cassell, London, 1996.
Rees, N., *Why Do We Say?*
    Blanford Press, London, 1987.
Rogers, J., *Dictionary of Clichés*,
    Angus & Robertson, London, 1986.
Room, A., *Brewer's Dictionary of Modern Phrase and Fable*,
    Cassell, London, 2000.
Room, A., *Place-Names of the World*,
    Angus & Robertson, London, 1987.
Sinclair, J. M., *Collins English Dictionary*, 4th Edition,
    HarperCollins, Glasgow, 1998.
Smith, C., *Alabaster, Bikinis & Calvados : An ABC of Toponymous Words*,
    Century Publishing, London, 1985.
Spiegl, F., *In Words and Out Words*,
    Elm Tree Books, London, 1987.
Sutton, C., *How Did They Do That?*
    Hilltown (Quill), New York, 1984.
The TIMES Book of Quotations,
    HarperCollins, Glasgow, 2000.
Thorne, Collocott (eds), *Chambers Biographical Dictionary*,
    Chambers, Cambridge, 1984.
Titelman, G., *America's Popular Proverbs and Sayings*, 2nd Edition,
    Random House, New York, 2000.
Tulloch, S., *Oxford Dictionary of New Words*,
    Oxford University Press, Oxford, 1991.
Walsh, W. S., *Handy-Book of Literary Curiosities*,
    Gibbings and Company, London, 1892.
Webster's Biographical Dictionary,
    Merriman Webster, Springfield, 1972.
Webster's New World Dictionary of the American Language,
    Collins & World, Cleveland, 1976.
Williams, T. (ed.), *Biographical Dictionary of Scientists*,
    HarperCollins, Glasgow, 1994.

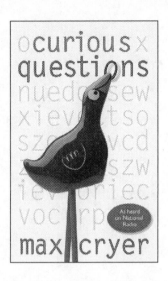

Curious Questions

What are bugger grips?
Why are potatoes called spuds?
What is the origin of the term redneck?
Was Sweet Fanny Adams ever a real person?

These and other curious questions have been sent to Max Cryer
for over three years, and every Saturday morning he has answered
them on National Radio with his customary wit and authority.
Now Max has compiled a book of questions (and answers!) from
the first three years of his popular 'Curious Questions' slot. The
questions focus on the quirks of the English language, the origins
of unusual words and popular expressions, and the particular way
in which New Zealanders use the language. Arranged alpha-
betically by key word, this book is a goldmine of information, to
be dipped into for reference or pleasure.

HarperCollins*Publishers*

Curious Kiwi Words

New Zealanders have their own lingo — favourite words and expressions which, although not always unique to this country, have been absorbed into our lives and become part of who we are. They include words that came with the early settlers or were coined by them in response to a new environment, words that travelled across the Tasman as a result of interaction with Australia, and Maori words that came to be part of our distinctive national vocabulary. In *Curious Kiwi Words* Max Cryer shares his favourite selection of words and phrases used by New Zealanders. From 'hangi' to 'gumboots', from 'give it heaps' to 'pack a sad', *Curious Kiwi Words* is chock-full of fascinating information for Kiwis and tourists alike.

HarperCollins*Publishers*

Curious Thoughts

A successful diet is the triumph of mind over platter.

The one good thing about egotists is that they don't talk about other people.

Best-selling author and entertainer Max Cryer returns with a compilation of his favourite sayings, used to conclude his 'Curious Questions' slot on National Radio each Saturday morning. From ageing disgracefully and the meaning of life, to pithy insults and musings on the perplexing nature of the English language, Max quips and puns his way through this delightful selection of aphorisms . . . or should we say 'maxims'?

HarperCollins*Publishers*